FAITH AND RELIGIOUS LIFE

A New Testament Perspective

FAITH AND RELIGIOUS LIFE
A New Testament Perspective

by
David M. Stanley, S.J.

PAULIST PRESS
New York / Paramus / Toronto

IMPRIMI POTEST:
Edward F. Sheridan, S.J.
Provincial, Province of Upper Canada

NIHIL OBSTAT:
J. Elliott MacGuigan, S.J.
Censor Deputatus

IMPRIMATUR:
✠ Francis V. Allen, D.D.
Auxiliary Bishop of Toronto

January 11, 1971

The Nihil Obstat and Imprimatur are official declarations that a book or pamphlet is free of doctrinal or moral error. No implication is contained therein that those who have granted the Nihil Obstat and Imprimatur agree with the contents, opinions or statements expressed.

Library of Congress
Catalog Card Number: 73-155846

Published by Paulist Press
Editorial Office: 304 W. 58th St., N.Y., N.Y. 10019
Business Office: Paramus, New Jersey 07652

Printed and bound in the
United States of America

Contents

For

FATHER JOSEPH P. MONAGHAN, S.J.,

my Master of Novices,

who long ago proposed to teach me

how to pray—

"as your mother and father know how to pray":

with affection and gratitude

Foreword

The substance of this little book was originally given as a series of lectures on the theme, "Faith and the Religious Life," for the religious women of Toronto and environs during November, 1970. The conferences were held at the request of the Reverend Angus J. Macdougall, S.J., Associate Vicar for Religious in the archdiocese of Toronto, and former president of the Canadian Religious Conference. The interest and enthusiasm of those who attended the talks in such impressive numbers moved the writer to make them available to a wider public, with the hope that they might prove of some assistance to other religious men and women in the common task of renewal set before us all by the Second Vatican Council.

It is just five years since Pope Paul VI closed Vatican II on December 8, 1965. During that relatively brief time much has been accomplished for the renewal and adaptation of the religious life within the Catholic Church. Still, one wonders whether the movement has now begun to lose momentum. Some, impatient of delays in institutional reform, are disillusioned to the point where abandonment of a religious vocation appears as the only alternative to fidelity to a way of life that seems incapable of adjustment to modern conditions. Others, indeed, with a nostalgic glance at what has been jettisoned of the traditional and the familiar in devotional and community life, voice their apprehension at what the future appears to hold in store for their survival as a congregation. And meanwhile, in the face of confusion, hesitation, division of opinion about the essentials of religious life, or the particular scope and distinctive aim of a given religious institute, fewer and fewer candidates present themselves at the door of the novitiate.

Yet there are many heartening indications that the travail so keenly felt in most religious institutes will issue in the re-

1

birth of a manner of life, at once loyal to a tradition that is centuries old and vibrantly responsive to the needs of contemporary man. One thinks with admiration of the new openness and courage in experimentation exhibited by senior as well as junior members of many congregations, of the growing mutual respect for one another being evinced in community dialogue, of a new-found sensitivity to the contemporary needs of the Church and of society at large. Perhaps one of the most striking signs of genuine renewal is the awakening of interest in, and concern for, their brothers and sisters who belong to other religious families.

Moreover, while our contemporary culture has created not a few problems for religious, it has also provided several significant helps. Sociology, psychology, historical research that is at once critical and creative, can offer a solid contribution to religious renewal and adaptation. More immediately, the renaissance during the past two decades of various theological disciplines, such as biblical studies, patristics, liturgy, and spirituality, is exercising its influence upon our understanding and esteem of the religious vocation.

The real work of religious renewal, however, must also be effected at a much deeper level—the level of our Christian faith. And here one is faced with a fundamental question: What is the nature and meaning of faith? As a concrete answer to this basic question, the first chapter of this book offers some reflections upon the gospel, as it is presented by the writers of the New Testament. Here it will quickly become evident how the impressive achievements of present-day theological scholarship may be enlisted as effective auxiliaries of religious renewal.

Two points in the development merit particular attention. First, there is the truth, attested by the inspired writers and reiterated in modern New Testament scholarship, that Christ's resurrection forms an integral part, together with his death, of man's redemption. The two greatest theological thinkers of the apostolic age, Paul and John, make this inseparable unity of Jesus' death and resurrection a pivotal point in their exposition of the gospel. Ever since the necessary vindication, in the sixteenth century, of the universally meritorious character of

Jesus' death laid stress upon the juridical and sacrificial aspects of his redemptive work, his resurrection was viewed preponderantly as the stamp of divine approval upon what had been accomplished by his Passion and death. This almost exclusive concentration upon one facet of the work of Christian salvation has left its mark on the theology of the Mass and the other sacraments. Its influence was also felt in devotional and ascetical practices, such as the Way of the Cross, reparation to the Sacred Heart, and penitential observances. It also obscured that equilibrated view of the religious life, in which the living of the evangelical counsels is regarded as the joyous celebration of Christian freedom.

Secondly, contemporary theology displays a more profound appreciation of what one might call the "good news value" of the gospel, that is, its unequivocal proclamation of divine love as the unique source of man's redemption in Christ. Nowhere in the New Testament is this divine economy ascribed to God's vindicative justice. The revalidation of this truth in contemporary spirituality must surely revolutionize our approach to the religious life.

No one is unaware, of course, that the renewal of religious life involves far more than an *aggiornamento* in theological thinking. At the same time it is imperative that a successful, authentic renewal adopt, as its point of departure, a truly Christian and integral vision of the world, of man in his historicity and in his relations with God, of God in his relation through Christ with man and the universe.

The second chapter is devoted to one of the vital and dynamic factors in the enterprise of religious renovation: prayer. Here it is a question of one aspect of prayer, germane to our general theme: its character as the expression of Christian faith. From this point of view, prayer appears predominantly as the believer's fundamental response to the divine summons to engage in the ongoing process of conversion announced by the gospel. Such response is of course solicited by God's initiative from every Christian, but the response of the religious should exhibit a specially intense, consistent, magnanimous quality. The prayer of faith postulates nothing less than total surrender of self from the man of faith, who places all his security in him, for whom "all things are possible" (Mk 10:27). A review of the chief obstacles to prayer serves to sharpen the uncompromising nature of the commitment by the religious to seek security only in the will of the heavenly Father. Since the religious life is orientated in a special way to the parousia of the risen Christ, it is the preoccupation with this mystery and its nearness, which provides grounds for the joy and security of the religious. "Rejoice in the Lord always! I say it again: rejoice! Let your magnanimity be manifest to all men— the Lord is near" (Phil 4:4-5). The contemporary phenomenon of a profound and universal interest in prayer is perhaps the first sign of the renewal of our religious life, which depends upon the vigor of our faith.

How does religious life, in its turn, serve as an aid to that faith which its very existence and survival demands? This is the question which the final chapter proposes to answer. The religious community by its basic, eschatological orientation to Christ's parousia, must perform a double task: that of untiring watchfulness for our Lord's second coming and that of alerting the Church not to relax its vigilance for the One who comes like a thief in the night. This means that religious life has been specially endowed with appropriate means to nourish that faith, which is the eye of Christian love for the coming Lord. The nature of the religious community as a paradigm (and in a true sense, an anticipation) of that new family redeemed by Christ, in which the will of God rather than the restrictive claims of clan or blood becomes the principle of solidarity, requires and continually assists the development of faith in its members. Indeed, the charismatic and prophetic character of religious life, which, while not belonging to the hierarchical structure, has nevertheless been accorded "the rights of the city" within the institutional Church, provides a further demonstration of the way religious life furthers the growth of faith. The charism of virginity, or chastity "in view of the kingdom of heaven," is a gift from God bringing a purification of heart and singleness of attention essential to faith. The charism of "common life," imbuing the religious with the zeal and energy for fraternal service, promotes the "faith made operative through love" (Gal 5:6). The charism of poverty lends assistance to faith by developing the sense of abandonment to God's providence, while the obedience, by which a religious submits himself to another human being, promotes faith as an effective symbol of man's complete submission of self to God.

It has not been the writer's intention to expand the treatment of the theme so as to cover completely this topic which is of paramount interest to the renewal and preservation of the religious life. Rather it was the hope that a presentation, inspired by some of the recent developments in New Testament scholarship, might illumine and revitalize certain motifs basic to the theology of the religious life, which have to a degree been operative in it from its origins.

It only remains to fulfill the very pleasant task of acknowledging my great indebtedness to two Canadian sisters, whose generosity in providing much discerning and constructive criticism of my manuscript merits a sincere vote of thanks. Each of these nuns belongs to a religious community that has figured prominently in the history of Canada. Sister M. St. Michael, O.S.U., is a daughter of the Venerable Marie de l'Incarnation; formerly dean of Brescia College, London, Ontario, she is now engaged upon a remarkable assignment in the Department of Social and Family Services for the provincial government of Ontario. Sister M. Eileen Scott, C.N.D., belongs to that gallant company of women founded by the Blessed Marguérite Bourgeoys. She is at present professor of English at Marianopolis College, Montreal and an authority on the life of the foundress of the Congregation of Notre Dame. The heartening fact that these two distinguished, very busy women accepted my appeal for help by criticizing the work with a simplicity and candor that matched their competence is, I should like to believe, symptomatic of "the new look" among religious women in our country. I am quite as grateful for their witness to this welcome phenomenon in religious life, as I assuredly am for their inestimable help.

Regis College, Willowdale, Ontario
January 25, 1971
Feast of the Conversion of Saint Paul

Chapter 1
The Foundations of
Christian Faith

The candidate who presents himself for admission to a religious community, we all realize, is led to take this significant step by Christian faith. During his noviceship, whatever else he may be presumed to master, he is surely expected to deepen his appreciation of the function of faith in his religious vocation. Today there is talk on all sides of the crisis of faith as the root cause of defections from the Church and from the religious orders. All Catholics, at least once a week, recite the Nicene Creed, which contains the chief articles of the Christian faith. Can we explain, in simple, concrete terms, in what the faith consists? Does the religious appreciate the impact, on his devotional and ascetical life, of his own personal vision of faith? It is with a view to obtaining a better insight into the relevance of faith for our lives as religious that we propose here to inquire into its foundations.

We may make a beginning by asking a basic question: Why do I believe? Why am I a Christian? The *immediate* answer is simply, because I trust the apostles, because I accept the testimony of the apostles. The word testimony is to be noted. Witnessing is a much more personal activity than proving, giving a demonstration. It involves not only the competence and knowledge of the one who attests: it involves him as a person. We conclude then that testimony is not mere "communications"; and Paul assures us that the apostolic testimony is not a question of rhetoric or closely reasoned argument (1 Cor 2:1-5), but of "the dynamic power of the Holy Spirit, carrying with it full conviction" (1 Thes 1:5). This leads us to probe deeper: Why *ultimately* do I believe? Because by God's gracious favor and through nothing in myself I am empowered to transcend myself and respond to God's call to become his son or daughter in Jesus Christ.

The testimony of the apostles, the immediate cause of my faith, is of course the gospel, the apostolic preaching. But, as Paul also reminds us, the gospel in its most existential meaning is "God's dynamic power leading to salvation" (Rom 1:16). Words may sway or convince a man: they cannot save him. The testimony of the apostles in itself may evoke my trust and confidence: it cannot save me. Only God's dynamic power can save. That divine power is the gospel. That truth is *the* foundation of faith. For it must not be forgotten that, while faith is my response to the gospel, it is not something of my own. It is, like the gospel, a wholly gratuitous, loving act of God's favor, his grace.

We might pause a moment to reflect that God's call, my Christian vocation, is a charism. As Paul says, it is *the* charism: "The charism is eternal life in union with Christ Jesus our Lord" (Rom 6:23). This free gift of God is always personal and individual: he calls me to be his son or daughter indeed. "You must be perfect as your heavenly Father is perfect," Jesus said (Mt 5:48). But that call or vocation brings concrete charisms with it, as for instance, the grace of Christian marriage, or the charism of religious life (1 Cor 7:7). To us who are religious God has freely given the charism which is common life, the charism which is virginity, the charism of poverty, of obedience. All these graces merely specify the *particular manner* in which we are to live out God's basic call to eternal life in union with Christ Jesus our Lord.

To return to the gospel, which I have called the foundation of our faith—it is that gospel which Vatican II has declared "is to be regarded by all religious institutes as their primary rule" (*Perfectae Caritatis*, n. 2a). Hence, we must now ask:

What is the gospel? What does it proclaim? The heart of the apostolic proclamation is the death and resurrection of Jesus Christ. And I venture to suggest that this proclamation can be set forth in its concrete significance by considering *seven aspects* of this good news.

The first thing I note is that the gospel proclaims *Jesus' death and resurrection as one event,* as two inseparable facets of one event, which constitutes the definitive saving act of God. We may well have become accustomed to thinking of our redemption only in terms of Jesus' atoning death; and indeed, since the Council of Trent, that emphasis dominated theological thought until the mid-twentieth century, and it still dominates much Christian spirituality. Yet how, if it proclaims the redemption solely, or even chiefly, through Jesus' sufferings and tragic death, can the gospel really mean "good news"? Our evangelists, as the Passion narratives clearly indicate, never forgot, nor allowed their readers to forget, that the resurrection of Jesus forms an integral part of God's saving action with his death. Paul is constantly aware of this twofold character of the foundation of Christian faith. "If we believe that Jesus died and rose, we also believe that God will bring those who have fallen asleep through Jesus together with him" (1 Thes 4:14). "To this purpose Christ died and rose: that he might be Lord both of dead and living" (Rom 14:9). He speaks moreover of "Jesus Christ who died, or rather, who was raised, who also intercedes on our behalf at God's right hand" (Rom 8:34). In fact, the Apostle describes Christian believers specifically as "those who believe in God, who raised our Lord Jesus from death—he, who was handed over for our sins and was raised for our justification" (Rom 4:25).

John has so clearly seen the necessary unity between Jesus' death and resurrection, that he can assert that the glorification of the risen Lord was inaugurated by his Passion. "When he [Judas] had taken his leave, Jesus said, 'Now is the Son of Man glorified, and God is glorified by him'" (Jn 13:31). Earlier in the Fourth Gospel, Jesus is represented as saying, "I lay down my life, in order to take it up again" (Jn 10:17). Such a candid avowal by Jesus that the purpose of his death is his own glorification has embarrassed some Catholic exegetes, who wish to defend Jesus here against any charge of egotism. Yet this expression of the causal sequence between Jesus' death and exaltation is surely deliberate on the part of the evangelist. John especially seeks to underscore the oneness of the paschal mystery, which was realized in Jesus himself by his passing from death to life.

This indissoluble unity of our Lord's death and resurrection is crucial to any real comprehension and true appreciation of Christian faith. It underscores the once-for-all character of Jesus' work of redemption. Paul has grasped this truth profoundly. "With regard to the death he died, he died to sin once for all: with regard to his present life, he lives unto God" (Rom 6:10). Jesus' death was definitive: his resurrection was definitive. He did not come back to life, as Lazarus, or the widow's son, or Jairus' daughter came back to *this* life, faced with the inevitable necessity of dying again. Jesus Christ has gone forward into life—a totally new existence with God his Father. His resurrection is unique, as his death is unique.

With regard to the character of Jesus' risen state (so difficult for us to imagine or comprehend, since it transcends all our experience), St. Thomas Aquinas makes a clear assertion. "The apostles saw the living Christ after his resurrection with the eyes of faith (*oculata fide*)" (*Summa Theologica,* III. 55. 2. ad 1). This remark is of paramount importance for understanding the role of faith in the meetings of the disciples with the risen Lord. St. Thomas certainly does not mean to imply that the risen Jesus was not bodily present, or that the truth of his resurrection merely consists in a subjective conviction by the first disciples that Jesus was again somehow alive. He does mean to insist man's natural senses cannot discern a glorified body without the aid of Christian faith. St. Thomas means to give an interpretation of the data provided by the Gospel narratives, which describe very concretely a set of experiences which almost defy description, but which explain adequately how the disciples received the gift of Christian faith.

When John represents Mary Magdalene as mistaking the

risen Jesus for a gardener (Jn 20:15), he is making the same
point as St. Thomas Aquinas. Whatever Mary may be thought
to have experienced at this phase of the encounter, she certainly did not see the risen Lord. It was only when, through
the gracious intervention of the glorified Jesus, she was granted
the grace of Christian faith, that she could recognize and
adore the incarnate Son of God (cf. vv. 16-17), and in the
sequel carry the "gospel" to the Twelve. Luke underscores
this same truth by his narrative of the meeting between the
risen Christ and the two disciples returning home to Emmaus.
Jesus appears to them at first as an ill-informed stranger
(Lk 24:18). It was only after he had "interpreted for them
what had befallen himself in the light of the entire Scriptures"
(v. 27), that "their eyes were opened and they recognized
him" (v. 31) in the breaking of bread. The narrative is an
attempt to describe the birth of Christian faith in the hearts
of Clopas and his unnamed companion.

St. Thomas Aquinas' observation, cited above, is meaningful
for another reason. It helps us to see the relationship between
our own faith-experiences of the risen Christ's presence in our
lives and those post-resurrection appearances of his to the disciples. These latter were indeed of a specially privileged nature,
inasmuch as they provided—together with those personal experiences of Jesus' public life—the basis for the gospel, the
testimony of the apostles, on which our own faith ultimately
depends. But they remained essentially experiences of Christian
faith, like our own experiences—a truth, which, when realized,
brings the Twelve much closer to us.

The oneness of Jesus' death and resurrection enables me
to grasp the nature of the sacraments. The Eucharist is the
sacrament of the risen body of Christ, who has become, as
Paul states, "life-giving Spirit" (1 Cor 15:45). For as John
observes, "It is the Spirit that is life-giver: the flesh profits
nothing!" (Jn 6:63). And St. Ignatius reminds us in the
Spiritual Exercises (n. 224) that now "it is the function of
consoler that Christ our Lord fulfills" in his risen life. He is
with me to console me. As for baptism, it is truly "baptism
into his death," as Paul characterizes it (Rom 6:4); but "we

were buried together with him through baptism into his death, in order that, just as Christ was raised from death through the glory of the Father, so we also might begin to live a new kind of life." The Eucharistic liturgy, as Paul perceived, is a proclaiming "of the death of *the Lord* [i.e., the risen Christ] until he comes" (1 Cor 11:26). It must be viewed as the joyful celebration of Christian freedom to which we have been called by God (Gal 5:1), that freedom won for us by Christ's death and resurrection.

It should now be clear that devotion to the Passion or any spirituality based upon the Passion must never be permitted to ignore the resurrection. It is not necessary, or even desirable, to add a fifteenth station to the Way of the Cross. It *is* imperative to contemplate the Passion in the light of Jesus' resurrection.

The second aspect of the gospel as the foundation of our faith may be stated thus. Jesus' redemptive act of mankind through death and resurrection is at the same time *the revelation of Jesus' unique relationship as Son to the Father,* a mystery which surrounded Jesus during his entire earthly life. This "Messianic secret," as scholars call it, was veiled from the disciples until, as a result of their post-resurrection experiences of the risen Lord, they received Christian faith. Only then were they enabled finally to penetrate the mystery of his person. Mark, who more than any evangelist dwells on this mystery surrounding Jesus in his public life, interprets Jesus' last cry as a shout of victory, presaging the resurrection. He represents the Roman centurion, who noted the distinctively different character of this cry of Jesus, as articulating the basic Christian act of faith. "The centurion . . . observing that he had died crying out as he did declared, 'Truly, this man was the Son of God' " (Mk 15:39).

Paul states this truth in a somewhat startling way, by saying of Jesus that "he was constituted Son of God in power by resurrection from the dead" (Rom 1:4). We may recall here that, in Paul's view, the meaning of the Incarnation lies in God's sending of his Son "in the likeness of sinful flesh" (Rom 8:3). "God made into Sin him, who knew no sin, in

order that we might in him become the Justice of God" (2 Cor
5:21). Paul has understood that the reality of the Incarnation
means that the Son, on becoming man, so identified himself
with the sinful family of the first Adam (insofar as that was
possible for one who was sinless), that in some real sense
the incarnate Son was alienated from the Father. Through
death and resurrection, Jesus Christ broke the ties binding
him to the sinful solidarity of the human race, and thus
deepened and enhanced his own Sonship, his unique relation
to God as his Father.

John recalls the revelation of Jesus' divinity and expresses
it through his characteristic concept of "exaltation." "When
you have lifted up the Son of Man, then you will know that
I AM" (Jn 8:28). Moses, commissioned by God to lead the
Hebrews out of Egypt, had asked God to tell him his name,
as a sign of his authorization for this difficult task. God replied,
"Tell them I AM has sent you to them" (Ex 3:14). Again,
in the Fourth Gospel Jesus states, "And I, when I am lifted
up from the earth, will draw all men to myself" (Jn 12:32).

The New Testament writers understood the ascension as an
integral part of Jesus' exaltation together with his resurrection.
They expressed their belief in his new life "lived unto God"
(Rom 6:10) with the help of Ps 110:1 by stating that Jesus
had taken his place "at God's right hand" (Acts 2:33; Heb
1:13). The hymn, cited by Paul in Phil 2:6-11, represents
Jesus at his exaltation as endowed with the divine name
Kyrios, that new name "at which every knee must bow." If
this truth is to be the foundation of our faith, however, we
must pierce the chrysalis of such an imaginative formulation
and arrive at its real meaning. For it does not imply that the
risen Jesus has become remote, that, having "traversed the
heavens" (Heb 4:14), he is (to use a slang expression) somehow "out of it." The apostles clearly perceived that Jesus'
ascension truly meant a more profound involvement with the
ongoing process of this world's history. They were keenly
aware that he was much more dynamically present among
them after his exaltation than ever he was when he walked
the hills of Galilee. That is why Matthew calls him "Emmanuel
—with us is God" (Mt 1:23), and records the promise of

the ascending Christ in the words: "Remember, I am with you throughout the course of history, until the consummation of this age" (Mt 28:20). The seer of Patmos in the opening vision of the Apocalypse pictures the risen Lord as walking among the golden lampstands (Apoc 1:13), as "holding in his right hand the seven stars" (v. 16) which symbolize "the angels of the seven churches," while "the seven lampstands are the seven churches" (v. 20). He has presented the dynamic quality of Christ's new presence as Master of history through the breaking of the seven seals (Apoc 6:1–8:2).

The evangelists are aware that the kingdom (reign, or dominion) of God was in fact already present to a degree in the earthly ministry of Jesus (Lk 11:20; 17:20-21). But as a consequence of Jesus' resurrection it was much more a contemporary reality, even though it always retained its incomplete character as an eschatological hope. The sacred writers are as conscious of the "not yet," as they are of the "already." Still their awareness that Jesus was now Lord of history provided them with a new insight into the meaning of our Lord's earthly history, enabling them to create the gospel. It is moreover this same insight which accounts for the remarkable lack of nostalgia for Jesus' earthly, mortal presence among them in "the days of his flesh" (Heb 5:7). The first Christians, who as Jesus' own disciples had enjoyed the deepest intimacy with him during his public ministry, never looked back to that period as a kind of vanished golden age to which they desired to return. This forward-looking attitude of the early Church, her absorption in contemporary history and her ever contemporary Lord, explains the essential orientation of the Church, away from the past, toward the present and the future. It also explains her continuing need of updating: for she must ever run to catch up with her Lord, who, as he promised, "goes before" her (Mk 14:28) as the very incarnation of *aggiornamento,* forever modern, forever up-to-date.

An appreciation of this truth can be seen in St. Ignatius' most characteristic method of prayer, his recipe for "finding God in all things."

The third aspect of the gospel is one we must consider

most attentively, since it has tended, because of certain polemic developments in the history of theology, to become obscured in Christian spirituality—even to the point of presenting a quite false idea of God in his dealings with us. The truth I refer to is this: that *Jesus' death and resurrection have revealed in its totality the marvel of God's love in his dealings with mankind.* The unfortunate representation of this divine economy in terms of God's justice—however necessary it may have been in an age of controversy—has left not a few Christians with a caricature of God the Father, as a sort of celestial Shylock, demanding his "pound of flesh" from man in the person of his own Son. The Gospel writers know nothing of this: in fact, the entire New Testament knows nothing of this.

We shall accordingly have to review the redemption as the disclosure in four distinct aspects of divine love: the love of the Father for sinful, rebellious man; the love of the incarnate Son for his estranged brothers; the love of the incarnate Son for the Father; and the love of the Father for the incarnate Son. We may note in passing that the love of Father for Son, of Son for Father as Person *is* the Holy Spirit, whose function in our redemption we shall presently discuss.

It surely must be obvious that if the gospel is truly good news it must announce Christian salvation as emanating from the love of God. Here I am reminded that my response of faith to the gospel must necessarily embrace love and obedience, which is the filial form of love. Inversely, the real nature of sin becomes evident: it is man's refusal to acknowledge who he is in relation to God—an adoptive son. Indeed, the original sin should be construed as the first parents' rebellion against this relationship as sons and daughters to the Father. This accords well with the views advanced by some modern theologians that original sin was essentially the refusal, on the part of the first man (or men), to create human society. The belief in the brotherhood of all men depends directly upon the belief in the universal Fatherhood of God.

We must first recall how Paul and John particularly insist that Jesus' death and resurrection spring from the love of God as Father of rebellious, sinful man. "God has fitted together a proof of his love, since, whilst we were still sinners, Christ died on our behalf" (Rom 5:8). "For I am convinced of this," Paul asserts, "that neither death nor life, nor angels nor the powers, nor the present nor the future age, nor [any forces of] height or depth, nor anything else in creation, will be able to separate us from the love God has shown in Christ Jesus our Lord!" (Rom 8:38-39). And John says, "By this we have come to know Love [i.e. God as Father: cf. 1 Jn 4:16, "God is Love"] because he [i.e. Jesus Christ] gave his life on our behalf" (1 Jn 3:16). "The love of God has been manifested to us by this, that God sent his only-begotten Son into the world in order that we might have life through him. This love consists, not in the fact that we loved God, but that he himself loved us, and sent his Son as propitiation for our sins" (1 Jn 4:9-10). Again, "God so loved the world as to give [over to death] his only-begotten Son, that every man with faith in him may not perish, but may possess eternal Life" (Jn 3:16).

The fact that the gospel presents God's offer of redemption as the initiative taken by a father vis-à-vis his rebellious sons explains Paul's habit of thinking of man's response to the gospel in faith as obedience. Man's acceptance of the divine gift by justifying faith must entail man's filial acknowledgment of his true relationship to God as his Father. Paul speaks of "the obedience of your faith" (Rom 1:5); he refers to his own missionary labors as "what Christ accomplished through me for the obedience of the Gentiles" (Rom 15:18). Thus we can see that, for Paul, faith is unintelligible without love. "In union with Christ Jesus, neither circumcision nor the lack of it has any force, but only faith made operative through love" (Gal 5:6). Here too we begin to understand the primacy of charity in Christianity. We must love one another because the Father and Christ first loved us, even "whilst we were still weak" and sinners, that is, when we were not lovable. Divine love is creative, as St. Augustine somewhere says, "By loving us, God makes us lovable." Finally, we may see the specific value of that fraternal love, which must be the basis and bulwark of any religious community. It is not, as in marriage, based on a personal, human relationship in the first place, but upon the receptiveness, the openness of genuine Christian love displayed toward a new candidate. *Congregavit nos in unum Christi amor!* Christ's love for us has gathered us together in fellowship.

It is probably worth repeating—as it certainly must be appreciated—that nowhere in the New Testament does this redemptive act of God the Father spring from any source except his love. No inspired author suggests that (as one might expect) it proceeded from divine justice, even though they are all very much aware of the incompatibility between God's holiness and man's sin. I venture to suggest that St. Thomas Aquinas did Christianity no great service, when he left the virtue of religion where the pagan Aristotle put it, under the category of justice.

The redemption also springs from the love of the incarnate Son for his sinful brothers and sisters—both in the theology of Paul and of John. For Paul, Jesus Christ remains "the Son of God who loved me, and handed himself over for me" (Gal 2:20). "For whilst we were still weak, at the decisive moment Christ died for us godless men. Why, a man will hardly give his life for an upright person!—though perhaps for a really good man someone might be brave enough to die" (Rom 5:6-7). And John presents Jesus as declaring, "Greater love than this no man has, that a man lay down his life for his friends. You are my friends . . ." (Jn 15:13).

How, in Paul's view, did Jesus actually redeem us? His death and resurrection were formally an act of loving obedience; for he accepted in all its concrete details the Father's plan to save mankind. Consequently, that death and resurrection was an act of love for rebellious man, since Jesus did what fallen man was, by definition, incapable of: he made for man the necessary act of acknowledging God as his Father. His love went ever further. Christ did not die and rise to exclude or even excuse man from making, for himself, this essential act of acknowledgment by which each man is redeemed. By dying and rising for man Christ created the possibility of man's offering his life to the Father as the final token of his filial love. Thus, in Christ, death became "a new creation." The Christian experience of death means that the Christian is empowered by Christ's grace to say "No" once-for-all to self, to his own life, by returning it as a gift into the hands of the Father, as Jesus himself did. "Father, into your hands I commend my spirit" (Lk 23:46). Moreover, this enables us to comprehend how the Eucharistic liturgy is truly a communal celebration of freedom—from sin and selfishness. Its position as the focal point of the life of any religious community as a foyer of Christian love is evident.

Jesus' death and resurrection is also announced in the gospel as a pledge of the incarnate Son's love for the Father. That is why Paul insists upon Christ's redemptive act as one of obedience to God. "He became obedient unto death, even death upon a cross!" (Phil 2:8). "By the obedience of the one Man the rest of men will be constituted upright" (Rom 5:19). When in Colossians Paul speaks of Christ as our redeemer, he characterizes him as "the Son of his [the Father's] love" (Col 1:13). "This is why the Father loves me," says Jesus in the Fourth Gospel, "because I lay down my life in order to take it up again. . . . This *command* have I received from my Father" (Jn 10:17-18). "But that the world may know that I love the Father," our Lord says to the disciples at the conclusion of the Last Supper, "Come! let us go from here" (Jn 14:31).

Finally, and perhaps strangely to us, the gospel presents Jesus' death and resurrection as proof of the Father's love for the incarnate Son. And here we encounter the obvious difficulty: How can any father who loves his son hand him over to death? Certainly, the objection is unanswerable if we think of the redemption as completed with Jesus' death. But Paul states that, if the Father "handed him over," he also "raised him" from death (Rom 4:25). Here we may recall the statement cited earlier, in which Paul asserts that Jesus Christ "was constituted Son of God in power by resurrection from the dead" (Rom 1:4). However, this aspect of the truth proclaimed in the gospel may be easiest appreciated, if we realize how both Paul and John employed the story in Genesis 22

(Abraham's sacrifice of Isaac) as a paradigm to express the good news of the Father's love for the incarnate Son in the very act of redeeming man. One should note that, in the narrative in Genesis, God is presented as chief agent both of the intended death of Isaac and of his deliverance. "Take your son, your only son, Isaac, whom you love . . . and offer him in sacrifice on the mountain I will show you" (Gen 22:2). Later, God stays the hand of Abraham: "Do not raise your hand against the boy. . . . Now I know you fear God, since you have not withheld your son, your only son, from me" (v. 12). Paul is thinking of this dramatic episode when he describes God the Father as the one "who did not even spare his own Son, but handed him over for the sake of us all" (Rom 8:32). John also recalls this story: "God so loved the world as to give [over to death] his only-begotten Son" (Rom 3:16; cf. 1 Jn 4:9).

I believe it may not be out of place, as we conclude this reflection on the redemption as a demonstration of divine love, to recall how Paul views the whole plan of God within the dimensions of the family. "We know that for those who love God he makes everything conspire to their good, for those called according to his plan. Because those he foreknew, he also predestined to be remolded in the image of his Son, so that he [the Son] might be the eldest of a large family of brothers" (Rom 8:29). We are reminded of a similar kind of statement in *Perfectae Caritatis* (n. 15). "Through the impact of God's love poured into hearts by the Holy Spirit (Rom 5:5), a religious community becomes a real family, gathered together in the Lord's name and filled with joy at his presence (cf. Mt 18:20)." A religious community is simply a collective attempt by a group of generous Christians to respond with complete single-heartedness to the call of the gospel.

The fourth aspect of the good news of man's redemption expressed by the gospel is this: by his death and resurrection, *Jesus Christ has become "the Way"* (Jn 14:6) *to the Father.* This optic is already perceptible in the Prologue to the Fourth Gospel, and is in fact characteristic of John. The Word become flesh has descended into man's history, in order to interpret to man "the God no man has ever seen" (cf. Jn 1:14-18). This disclosure, initiated in the unique life of Jesus of Nazareth, is finally effected by Jesus' return to the Father. The way Jesus has traversed is the way the believer must travel home to the Father; and the means provided to assist man on his way are "the signs," that is, the mysteries of Jesus' earthly life offered by John for Christian contemplation, and those other "signs," the Christian sacraments. Thus, where Paul presents Christ's work as an act of *redemption,* John views it rather as an act of *revelation.* As a revelation-event, Jesus' death and resurrection discloses who Jesus is, the Lord of history (Jn 20:28), who God is, our Father (Jn 14:9) and, in a unique sense, "the Father of our Lord Jesus Christ" (Jn 10:30; 17:11). It also discloses who man is in his historicity—a rebellious son of the Father he does not know (Jn 8:19, 54).

Faith in this revelation-context signifies, for John, a kind of vision, an experiential awareness of God as Father which is present in the believer, imbued with "the power to become a child of God" (Jn 1:12), who thus "sees the Son" in Jesus (Jn 6:40) by means of "the signs" narrated in the Gospel. For such a man, who already possesses "eternal life" (Jn 3:16), Christ is most truly "the Way." In Paul's thought, which moves in the context of redemption, the risen Christ has, as "the last Adam," become "life-giving Spirit" (1 Cor 15:45) and "the image of God" (2 Cor 4:4; Col 1:15). Accordingly, man, as a result of faith and baptism, is now being remolded in the image of the Son (2 Cor 3:18; Rom 8:29). Paul, as a consequence, considers Christian faith as an interpersonal relationship with Christ, the result of man's total commitment of self to his redeemer in this life (Gal 2:20). Faith is also the expression of man's obedience to God (Rom 1:15) and the source of his true security, permitting him to "boast in God through our Lord Jesus Christ, through whom we have now received the reconciliation" (Rom 5:11).

If Paul does not depict the risen Christ as "the Way," he nevertheless describes the Christian life-style as patterned upon continual participation in Jesus' death and resurrection, as a series of crises, dyings and risings. Paul's prayer is "that I may know him and the power of his resurrection and fellowship in his sufferings, being molded to the pattern of his death, in order to arrive, if possible, at the resurrection from death" (Phil 3:10-11). "We are continually bearing the dying of Jesus in our person, in order that the life of Jesus also may be manifested in our person: for always we the living are being handed over to death for Jesus' sake, in order that Jesus' life may be manifest in our mortal flesh" (2 Cor 4:10-11; cf. Col 1:24).

John approaches this Pauline conception in the brief parable in Jn 12:24. "Unless the grain of wheat when thrown into the ground dies, it remains in isolation. But if it dies it produces great fruit." In the context, it is clear that Jesus refers to his own participation in the paschal mystery. But, as the sequel indicates, this "Way" through death to life must be followed by the disciple. "The man who loves his life is destroying it: the man who hates his life *in this world* will guard it for eternal life. If a man serves me, he must follow me; and where I am there also my servant will be: if a man serves me, my Father will honor him" (vv. 25-26). There is one point on which both Paul and John agree, since they are both disciples of Jesus who taught the same doctrine (cf. Mk 8:34-35): the Christian goal is *not* self-fulfillment—it is self-transcendence.[1]

To make John's conception of Jesus as "the Way" effective and operative in one's spirituality, one should see that it points to the supreme paradox contained in the gospel—that the risen Christ has chosen to remain human forever. The author of Hebrews has caught this sense of paradox: "Jesus Christ, yesterday and today the same—and so forever!" (Heb. 13:8).

---

[1] The distinction between self-fulfillment and self-transcendence may strike the reader as contrived, a mere *lis verborum*. It is true indeed that genuine self-fulfillment *is* self-transcendence. We can never afford to forget, however, the uncompromising manner with which Jesus insisted upon the disciple's saying "No" to self (Mk 8:34). If there is any recorded saying of Jesus that is authentic, it is surely this most uncomfortable one!

As the great St. Teresa of Avila and St. Ignatius so emphatically insist: there is no way to God except through the glorified humanity of the Son. Any other spirituality, as St. Teresa learned to her cost, is deceptive and dangerous. Moreover, this truth tells me that any spirituality that would seek to dehumanize man is suspect and bogus. And here I recall that the inhuman par excellence is selfishness, making self supreme.

Again, as "the Way," the risen Lord has created the Christian pattern *through death to life,* a pattern which must finally be allowed to stamp the character of genuinely Christian asceticism; and this can never be merely negative. We must die to self in order to open self to other human beings, and so ultimately to God our Father in life. It is an open secret that many young religious reject the traditional forms of ascetical practice. Are they perhaps not telling us that these have been less than meaningful because negative, less than Christian because Stoic?

Since the risen Christ remains man as "the Way," every authentically human institution, each genuine manifestation of the human spirit, is necessarily of concern to the Christian. He is in fact impelled toward this concern by his *faith!* He is led to view these products of human culture as revelations of the hidden, yet very real, dynamic presence of the Lord of history. He is enabled to perceive the missionary experience as primarily of benefit to the preacher of the gospel in foreign, pagan lands. He sees that the missionary must experience Christ's presence in that culture, in the institutions (even religious) of pagan peoples. Indeed, it will only be as a consequence of this vision springing from his Christian faith that the missionary can effectively preach the gospel "to all the nations."

This truth that the glorified Jesus retains his humanity as Lord of history provides a profounder insight into the meaning of his resurrection. Christian faith tells me that not only has he gone forward into the new "life unto God" with his body, but he has also carried with him that sum of human experiences which we call his earthly life. This is the importance of the central symbol in the Apocalypse depicting

the glorified Master of history as "a Lamb standing with the
marks of his slaying upon him" (Apoc 5:6). Jesus in glory
still wears the badges of his sacred Passion! The very modality
of his Lordship has been determined by his Passion and death
—and by his whole earthly life. Christ is Lord *as he now is*
in virtue of all the experiences of his existence upon earth.
And because that means, as well, that these human experiences, the mysteries of his mortal life, have acquired a new
actuality in and through his resurrection, they constitute him
"the Way" to God. Hence it must be through these mysteries
as presented in the gospel that the Christian feeds his life of
faith, his prayer-life. It is this insight of faith, enshrined in the
Spiritual Exercises, that has won for it the universal acclaim
as "a golden little book."

The fifth aspect of the proclamation of Jesus' death and
resurrection in the gospel is the significant fact that *the Holy
Spirit is the gift of the risen Lord Jesus.* In the thought of
Paul, the Spirit has two essential functions in Christian living:
one in this present life, and one which prepares for our entry
into the life to come. In this life, the Holy Spirit provides
the Christian with the possibility of *experiencing in prayer*
the truth of his divine adoptive sonship. In the future life,
the Spirit will bring that adoptive sonship to its culmination
by his activity in the glorious resurrection of the just. With
regard to the Spirit's function in contemporary Christian existence, Paul says: "When the fullness of time was come, God
sent his Son . . . in order that we might receive the adoptive
sonship. The proof that you are sons is the fact that God has
sent the Spirit of his Son into your hearts calling, 'Abba!
(dear Father!)'" (Gal 4:4-6). Again, "Those who are led
by the Spirit of God are sons of God. You have not received
a spirit of slavery [leading you back] again into fear. No,
you have received the Spirit of adoptive sonship by which we
call 'Abba! (dear Father!)'" (Rom 8:14-15). Paul adds,
"The Spirit comes to the aid of our weakness, since we do
not know how to pray as we ought," that is, to learn conformity with the Father's will (Rom 8:26).

With regard to the second, *eschatological function* of the

Spirit in effecting man's resurrection, Paul has this to say. "If the Spirit of him who raised Jesus from death dwells in you, the one who raised Christ from death will also bring your mortal bodies to life through his Spirit dwelling within you" (Rom 8:11). Thus the Spirit becomes "the Spirit of our adoptive sonship" in a twofold sense. He reveals to the believer the mystery of his relationship to the Father as an adopted son through the experience of Christian prayer. However, this divine adoption, although a reality in the present life, is not yet brought to its full perfection, in Paul's view. This is clear from his statement about the glorified Jesus, that he "was constituted Son of God in power by resurrection from the dead" (Rom 1:4), even though, as pre-existent Christ, he was Son of God from all eternity. We have already taken cognizance of the fact that, for Paul, the unique relationship of the incarnate Son to the Father was deepened and enhanced by his exaltation. This is much more profoundly true of the Christian's *adoptive* filiation, and hence Paul can state that "we also, although we possess the first fruits of the Spirit, are groaning to ourselves as we await our adoptive sonship" (Rom 8:23).

In the theology of John, the office of the Holy Spirit, gift of the risen Christ, is to be "another Paraclete," that is, another defense-counsel. Jesus is the first Paraclete, but at his "going away" to the Father he is to be replaced in the lives of the disciples by the Holy Spirit. John states clearly, first of all, that Jesus, when glorified, is the source of the Spirit. " 'If any man thirsts,' Jesus cried, 'let him come to me and drink— I mean, the man with faith in me! As Scripture has it, "From his Heart will flow fountains of living water." ' Jesus said this with reference to the Spirit, whom those with faith in him were going to receive. The Spirit was not yet, since Jesus was not yet glorified" (Jn 7:37-39). Because, in John's view, Jesus is glorified upon the cross, he is pictured by that evangelist as imparting the Spirit with his dying breath. "And bowing his head, he handed over the Spirit" (Jn 19:30). The risen Jesus bestows it upon the disciples at his first appearance to them. "When Jesus had said this, he breathed into them, and said to them: 'Receive the Holy Spirit—whose sins you shall remit, they remain remitted . . .' " (Jn 20:22).

In the discourse after the Last Supper, which John probably created with the help of the truths conveyed to the disciples through the post-resurrection appearances, Jesus tells the Twelve, "I will ask the Father, and he will give you another Paraclete to be with you forever: the Spirit of Truth. You will recognize him because he will remain with you and be in you. I shall not leave you orphans: I will come back to you" (Jn 14:16-18). "The Paraclete, the Holy Spirit, whom the Father will send in my name, will teach you everything and recall to your minds all I have said" (Jn 14:26). "When the Spirit whom I shall send you from the Father comes, the Spirit of Truth who proceeds from the Father, he will bear witness concerning me . . ." (Jn 15:26). "I tell you the truth: it is to your [spiritual] profit that I go away. If I do not go away, the Paraclete will not come to you; yet if I go away, I will send him to you" (Jn 16:7). "And when he comes, the Spirit of Truth, he will lead you into the full range of truth" (Jn 16:13). In the Apocalypse, it is through the Spirit that the risen Christ as contemporary judge of the Church speaks to the various communities (Apoc 2:7, etc.).

It is perhaps well to recall that the gift of the Spirit is thought of as bestowed first of all upon the collectivity, which is the Church or the community (1 Cor 3:16; 6:19). Paul and John are not unaware of the indwelling of the Spirit in the individual Christian; but as semites nourished by the Old Testament they tend to think first of the Spirit's indwelling in the community. As a religious I ought to reflect upon this community aspect of the bestowal of God's grace. The graces relative to my religious vocation come to me through the community.[2]

[2] That is to say, the particular religious family provides the general context in which the individual religious receives those charisms from God, which constitute him a *bona fide* member of this, rather than some other, community. Within this rather broad frame of reference, however, there is ample room for individual and quite distinctive charisms. A Jesuit naturally thinks of the singular divine gifts exhibited by Gerard Manley Hopkins or Pierre Teilhard de

Paul particularly insists upon the role of the Spirit in the Christian's quest for self-identity. The Spirit makes me aware through faith of *who I am* (Rom 8:16), that is, a son or daughter of the Father. He alerts me to the truth that all men and women are members of the one family of God. And it is the Spirit (Rom 8:15) who gives me the power to act as son or daughter of God. He does this chiefly in my prayer, by helping me experience personally this familial relationship. As the Spirit takes me "out of myself" constantly in this life, he will effect the fullest self-transcendence in me at the resurrection of the just. Only then will my adoptive sonship be perfectly realized.

We may recall, in passing, the sense of the term *spiritual* in Scripture. It is not, as with us, opposed to the material; rather it signifies whatever is under the domination of the Holy Spirit. My spiritual life is not something apart from the material aspect of my human existence. St. Ignatius realized this clearly in his *Rules for the Discernment of Spirits* (cf. especially nn. 316, 317, 333, 334). The "spirits" of which he speaks are my own personal reactions to everything which affects me as a living person: not only my thoughts, will-acts, but my emotions, my imagination as well. His point is that, by becoming aware of these reactions within myself I can learn Christian prudence, the ability to discern the will of God in each situation in which I find myself. He is aware that the Spirit of God speaks to me through myself, that is, through these various "spirits," or reactions in my conscious life. In themselves they are ambiguous: they may come from the power of evil, or from the Holy Spirit. The judicious discernment and correct evaluation of these reactions, however, is the

---

Chardin. Yet each of these religious clearly reveals a vision of faith recognizably the same as that of the author of the *Spiritual Exercises*. My religious vocation is simply a specific set of charisms similar to other members of my religious family, who share with me the enterprise inspired by the vision of our religious founder. My community can, in virtue of the similar structure of the gifts bestowed upon all its members, assist my response to the grace of my particular vocation by accepting me initially and by continuing to accept me as one in whom they perceive a similar pattern of graces.

ordinary means of hearing the voice of the Spirit revealing to me the will of God.

The sixth aspect of the gospel is one perhaps that is not as well known or appreciated. By his death and resurrection *Jesus Christ has redeemed not only man, but also the material creation.* The idea that our world is doomed to total annihilation is a Stoic, not a Christian notion. The irrational creation shares with man a destiny in the world to come: it is not doomed to destruction, it is destined to transformation. "We expect," says the author of 2 Peter, "a new sky and a new earth according to his promise, in which justice will dwell" (2 Pt 3:13). Thus the vision of Christian faith necessarily includes the world of *things.* "And I beheld a new sky and a new earth," says the seer of Patmos, "for the former sky and former earth had disappeared, and the sea no longer existed" (Apoc 21:1). "And he who is seated upon the throne said, 'Lo! I make all things new' " (Apoc 21:5). God almost never speaks in the Apocalypse: he is represented as doing so here to announce the transformation of the cosmos.

In his last letters, Paul speaks continually of this cosmic aspect of the redemption. For in Christ "it was God's good pleasure that the whole universe might dwell and that through him he might reconcile all things to himself, by making peace, through his blood [shed] on the cross, among all things, whether upon earth or in heaven" (Col 1:19-20). "To bring all things under one head in Christ" is the way Ephesians 1:10 describes the divine "mystery of his will." Paul dwells upon this theme in Romans 8:18-22: "For I reckon that the sufferings we now endure bear no comparison with the glory, as yet unrevealed, which is in store for us. The created universe waits with eager expectation for the revelation of the sons of God. It was made the victim of frustration, not by its own choice, but through him who made it so. Yet always there was hope, since the creation itself is to be freed from the shackles of mortality, and is to enter upon the freedom of the glory of the children of God. Until the present moment, we know, the whole created universe is groaning in all its parts as with the pangs of childbirth."

Man's redemption, then, is interlocked with the redemption of the material creation. That self-transcendence, which we have seen to be the goal of Christian perfection proposed by the gospel, *does not mean transcendence of the material.*[3] Man is not saved *from* this world; he is not redeemed, as a kind of purely spiritual being, *out of* matter. It is not technically correct to speak, as we do, of "saving our souls." Redemption in Christ does not rupture man's solidarity with the material.

It is historical man who is the object of salvation in Christ: man in his historicity, with his sins and failures, as also with his artistic and scientific achievements, the work of his own hands. It does then make a profound difference for eternity whether man succeeds in splitting the atom, in subduing and directing the forces of nature, in producing the great masterpieces of art, and music. For indeed, it is in this way—as the priestly editor of Genesis clearly saw—that man is to authenticate that "image and likeness of God," after which he was fashioned in the beginning (Gen. 1:26). In the mind of this inspired author, the peremptory summons of man by God, to exercise responsibility in the world of irrational creatures, indicates the way in which man is to grow into the divine "image" in which he was created. "Be fruitful and multiply: fill the earth and subdue it; exercise dominion over the fishes in the sea, the birds in the sky, and every living thing that moves on the face of the earth" (Gen 1:28).

This teaching of Genesis, reinterpreted by Paul in relation to Christ, informs the Christian that it is not enough to do a poor job with a pure intention. In the Christian vision of history, there are no small tasks—even though there may be small minds.

"After we have, with the spirit of Christ and in obedience to his command, cultivated upon earth those goods belonging to the dignity of man, to his brotherly solidarity, and to

---

[3] This significant item of good news in the gospel must not be allowed to slip into oblivion today, as has happened not infrequently in the past. Surely the history of the Church bears abundant witness that "angelism" is only a thinly disguised form of Manicheism.

his liberty—that is to say, the blessings of nature, as well as of our own enterprise—we shall rediscover them once more, when Christ returns the . . . kingdom to the Father, cleansed of all dross, radiantly pure, and transformed" (*Gaudium et Spes*, n. 39). This conception of the Church in the modern world, defined by Vatican II, deserves to be pondered deeply by all religious engaged upon the work of spiritual renewal, for it adopts a world view that has not always functioned effectively in Christian spirituality. "We are warned, it is true," this same passage states, "that a man can gain nothing by acquiring the entire world at the cost of losing himself. At the same time, the expectation of the new earth should not dampen, but rather stimulate concern for cultivating this present world. . . . Earthly progress is never to be confused with the growth of Christ's kingdom. Still such progress is of vital interest to the kingdom of God, insofar as it can contribute to the better ordering of human society." Here we are given a deeply Christian theology of work, that has drawn its inspiration from the Pauline conception of the cosmic redemption. Man has been challenged by God in Christ to participate responsibly in the redemption of the entire universe.

The seventh, and final, aspect of the gospel, which proclaims the Lordship of Jesus Christ through his death and resurrection, *presents that Lordship as a piece of unfinished business*. Jesus risen is now Master of history, but, as the first Christians well knew, he is deeply involved with the ongoing process of history, because his exaltation as Lord is still incomplete. "He must reign as king," says Paul, "until he has set all his enemies beneath his feet. The last enemy to be destroyed will be Death . . . and when everything has been made subject to him, then the Son himself will be subject to him, who subjected all things to him—that God may be all in all" (1 Cor 15: 25-28). The Apocalypse presents the same theme in somewhat more dramatic fashion: only at the termination of history will the victorious Lamb, the Word of God, assume his proper title "King of kings and Lord of lords" (Apoc 19:16).

It is this very unfinished character of Jesus' Lordship which once summoned the Church into existence. Moreover, it reveals the meaning of the Christian's vocation: he is summoned by God in Christ (to paraphrase Paul) in order "to fill up what is lacking" in the Lordship of Jesus. Here then is the real reason why Christian faith demands concern with man's history. The heartening truth is that *Jesus Christ now risen is not yet what he will be*. This enables us to grasp somewhat more clearly the meaning of the parousia, the second coming. For our faith tells us that, as Master of history, our Lord is already present, in a deeply involved and dynamic manner, in the lives of every one of us. How then can he be said "to be coming"? The parousia does not primarily herald the end of history, but the completion of the exaltation of Christ himself.

Thus I realize that my Christian faith, in addition to embracing love, must also include hope. The object of Christian hope is "he who comes": it is a growing hope, an expanding hope, as long as history continues. Christ's mysterious second coming must be seen as a *becoming*. That is why, ultimately, it is of the very essence of hope that it transcend the present moment, both in my own life and in the history of the world and in the evolution of Jesus Christ himself. Paul saw that with reference to his own "justification," his own spiritual development, as well as with reference to Jesus' Lordship. "By the Spirit," he writes to the Galatians, "we await out of faith the hope of justification" (Gal 5:5). This truth points to the element of risk to which the Christian by vocation is called. On this venturesome journey, the author of Hebrews suggests, we should do well to choose Abraham as patron. "By faith Abraham obeyed the call to emigrate to a country destined as a heritage; and he left home without knowing where he was going. . . . For he was looking forward to the city erected on solid foundations, whose architect and builder is God" (Heb 11:8-10). This sacred writer praises a whole "cloud of witnesses" (Heb 12:1), whose faith led them on in hope. "They had not yet come into possession of the things they had been promised, but had only glimpsed them from afar and hailed them. . . . If they had left their hearts in the country they had abandoned, they would have had ample opportunity of turning back. In point of fact, however, they were longing for a better country—I mean, the heavenly one. That is why God was not ashamed to be invoked as their God; for he had readied a city for them" (Heb 11:13-16).

Chapter 2
Prayer as
Expression of Faith

We have seen that faith is the Christian response to God's initiative, concretely embodied and presented to man historically in the life of Jesus Christ. This totally free and gracious offer from God our Father in his incarnate Son was made principally and definitively through our Lord's death and resurrection. That two-faceted event was the mediating action of God's self-revelation as "our Father and the Father of our Lord Jesus Christ" (Phil 1:2), as it was also of man's redemption. Hence, as the act of man's *redemption,* it is a summons to participate in the paschal mystery. From this aspect, Christian faith appears as an interpersonal relationship with Christ the redeemer, once dead and now "alive forevermore" (Apoc 1:18) with "the life he lives unto God" (Rom 6:10). As an act of God's *self-revelation,* the Christ-event is an invitation to self-awareness on the part of man. Seen from this angle, the Christian's faith is an ever deepening consciousness of who he is, a son of God by adoption and brother to all other human beings.

Yet this historical divine call to faith is communicated to man in his historicity, that is, to fallen man. Hence Christian faith is also basically a summons to repentance (*metanoia*), to a deep, personal reorientation to God in Christ of man's existence, his values, his actions and reactions, "with his whole

heart, and his whole life, and his whole mind, and all his
strength" (cf. Lev 19:18 as cited in Mk 12:30). From this
aspect the response of faith cannot be made without prayer:
in fact, such faith is prayer. We may note here in passing
also that such a response to God's imperious invitation to
change involves *risk*. For Jesus himself ran the supreme risk
(such was the Father's will) by entering the solidarity of the
sinful human race, so far as that was possible for him, who
remained sinless. This hazardous enterprise came to its climax
in Jesus' death and resurrection. Is not this aspect of Jesus'
response to the Father portrayed by Mark in his articulation
of Jesus' cry, "My God, my God! why have you forsaken
me?" (Mk 15:34; cf. also Mt 27:46). Is not the same risk
implicit in the statement found in Paul, that Jesus "emptied
himself, by adopting the character of the Servant" (Phil 2:7)?
The author of Hebrews, in his turn, appears to be aware of
the hazardous nature of our redemption, when he states of
Jesus that "in the days of his flesh, with a mighty cry and
tears, he offered prayers and supplications to him who could
save him from death" (Heb 5:7).

Because the divine summons to the believer involves such
a radical reorientation of himself, because its realization in
any human life entails such risk, God has graciously provided
man with a pattern and a paradigm in this hazardous under-
taking through the narratives, found in the four Gospels, of
the earthly history of Jesus Christ. And still, as we have seen,
these inspired narratives do not present merely the dear mem-
ories of a dead past, in the way in which the Dialogues of
Plato preserve a grateful pupil's reminiscences of a dead master, Socrates. They rather provide a living pattern by offering
to Christian faith the insight into the mysteries, once veiled
by Jesus' earthly history, and now endowed, in the risen Jesus,
with a new contemporaneity and a new relevance for Christian existence. From this vantage point, faith manifests itself
as a divine summons to contemplate the human history of
Jesus Christ, who in his exaltation appears before man as
"the Way" to the Father.

It may be helpful, finally, to recall that my response of

faith is itself a gracious gift of God to me in my own unique historical individuality. God's free, untrammelled, deliberate choice falls upon me as a person, which is the biblical meaning of *election*. "You have not chosen me; rather, I have chosen you" (Jn 15:16), Jesus said to the Twelve. This divine choice, my Christian vocation, contains all the charisms necessary for Christian living, and this, in the specific manner determined by God, for example, my religious life. One charism, of the many which go to make up my religious life, is pre-eminent: the grace of prayer. Indeed, my individual calling as a religious in a particular religious institute, my lifelong commitment of myself to God as my Father in Christ, *is* prayer in its basic reality. At the same time it may be said that prayer is necessary, just because it is a particular and special gift of God to me as part of my call to be a religious, for the full realization of my individual identity as a religious man or woman. As we shall see from a brief review of Old Testament and New, it is imperative that I *remember* all God's gracious actions in my regard. Of none is this so necessary as the remembering that particular personal gift, my vocation— to be a Christian by being a religious.

In fact, so allied to a specific religious vocation is the distinctive charism of prayer, that it becomes possible, at least in certain instances, to characterize a particular religious vocation in terms of a special prayer-structure which formed a notable part of the charism given a religious founder. This is certainly true of the vocation to the Society of Jesus. I venture to speak of it here, not merely because I may be better acquainted with it than the vocation to other religious orders, but also because it may be said to be a formative element in the prayer characteristic of a good number of religious families, whose spirituality is drawn in some degree from the Ignatian *Exercises* and *Constitutions*. In the notes which Father Jerome Nadal composed on the *Examen Generale,* the document defining for a prospective candidate the Jesuit way of life, this distinguished early companion of St. Ignatius makes the following assertion:

"Father Ignatius, we know, received from God the unique

grace of great facility in the contemplation of the most Holy
Trinity. This gift of contemplative prayer he received in a
very singular manner toward the end of his years on earth,
although he had enjoyed it frequently also at other times. At
that period, however, he possessed it to such a degree that
in all things, in every action or conversation, he was aware
of God's presence and felt so great a taste for spiritual things
as to be lost in their contemplation. In a word he was *simul
in actione contemplativus* (contemplative even while engaged
in activity), a habit he was accustomed to explain by re-
marking: 'God must be found in all things.'

"Now we believe that this same privilege, which we are
aware was bestowed on Father Ignatius, has been accorded
to the whole Society. We feel certain that in the Society this
grace of contemplative prayer awaits all of us. We declare it
has been joined to our vocation." [1]

Father Nadal describes the prayer-style of the Jesuits by
saying in another passage, "The prayer characteristic of the
Society is orientated to action." [2] Elsewhere he explains the
meaning of his remark: "This is what I should like to call
the cycle of occupations in the Society. If you are occupied
with your neighbor and with the service of God in your ministry
or in any assigned task, God will help you afterward more
efficaciously in your prayer. And this more effective divine
aid will in turn enable you to take care of your neighbor with
more courage and spiritual profit." [3]

Thus the *structure* of the Jesuit's prayer-life is patterned
upon the specific form assumed by St. Ignatius' singular grace
of infused contemplation, and this quite distinctive style of
prayer is part of God's call to the Society. It is surely obvious
that Nadal does not mean that all Jesuits are graced with the
specially privileged kind of prayer, infused contemplation,
conferred upon their founder. He does however insist that the

[1] *Monumenta Historica Societatis Iesu, Epistolae P. Hieronymi
Nadal, IV* (Madrid, 1905), 651-652.
[2] M. Nicolau, *Jeronimo Nadal, Obras y Doctrinas Espirituales*
(Madrid, 1949), 307.
[3] Cf. M. Nicolau, *op. cit.,* 324-325.

particular modality that characterized that mysticism has impressed a distinctive stamp upon the charism of prayer offered to those called to the Society of Jesus. It is, if you like, a "worldly" mystique, this practice of "finding God in all things." It is admittedly a quite "practical"—there are those who have called it "pragmatic"—spirituality, which discovers in the work assigned for the Jesuit's day-to-day living, the *normal* object and incentive of his prayer. It is, most certainly, "evangelical," in that it seeks to respond to the challenge of the gospel to find one's personal point of insertion into contemporary salvation-history by "finding God in all things," as the consequence of contemplating the dynamic presence of the risen Lord of history.

These introductory observations on that specific response of faith, the acceptance of God's call to religious life, indicate the format of our reflections upon prayer as expression of our Christian faith. Here again there are seven aspects of this topic which we must take into consideration. However, I suggest that we begin by recalling the principal obstacles to prayer, which, I judge, are four in number.

The crudest form of the wrong approach to God in prayer is exemplified in *the pagan attitude to sacrifice*. The gods of the Gentiles were nature gods, personifications of the forces of nature, which man has ever sought to control. These whimsical, unpredictable deities must be manipulated by the worshiper through coercion, bribery, or persuasion. This offering of sacrifice was calculated to make the god indebted to man, or to win his favor to "propitiate" him. It is significant that nowhere in the Bible is the believer said to propitiate God. There is no least suggestion that man can win the divine pleasure by any means other than his change of heart—itself a free gift of God. The prophets of Israel consistently and often vehemently insist that sacrifice has significance only as the expression of the covenant-relationship with God. Samuel excoriates Saul for ignoring this truth at Gilgal:

Does the Lord take the delight in holocausts and sacrifices that he takes in obedience to his command?

> Remember, obedience is better than sacrifice:
> compliance, better than the fat of rams.
> Rebellion is sinful as sorcery,
> presumption is wicked as idolatry.
> (1 Sam 15:22-23)

The first Isaiah (Is 1:11-17) inveighs against the substitution of sacrifice for social justice, and includes explicitly all superstitious recourse to prayer in lieu of real conversion:

> When you plead with hands outstretched in prayer,
> I will hide my eyes from you.
> Though you utter interminable prayers,
> I will not listen.
> Your hands have blood upon them—
> wash yourselves, make yourselves clean!
> (Is 1:15-16)

This tendency to reduce the cult of God to magic springs from a misapprehension of the nature of God himself, particularly of his absolute freedom in dealing with man. Judith upbraids the magistrates of Bethulia for their decision to surrender within five days to the Assyrian besiegers, unless God sent some relief: "Who then are you to test God in a crisis like this, and set yourselves above God publicly? . . . How can you fathom God, predict his mind, or divine his thought? No, my brothers, stop rousing the Lord our God to anger! Even if he does not decide to assist us within the five days, he is perfectly free to rescue us at any time he pleases, or to bring us down in the face of our enemies. It is not for you to impose conditions on the plans of the Lord our God; God does not yield to threats like a man, nor can he be bargained with like a mere human. Consequently, we must wait for him to deliver us, and in the meantime appeal to him for help. If he deems it best, he will hear us" (Jud 8:12-17). In the Sermon on the Mount, Jesus deprecates this pagan attitude toward prayer: "When you are praying, do not prattle on like pagans: they think they will win a hearing by sheer force of words. Do not imitate them. Your Father realizes what you need before you ask him" (Mt 6:7-8).

The crassness of this attitude is of course obvious, and one may well ask why it is even mentioned. It does serve, however, as a graphic illustration of our theme that prayer must be the expression of authentic faith in God. It also reminds us religious of the need we always have of purifying our own image of God through prayer. I can never permit myself to forget that God, in his dealings with me, is always the one infinitely free Being. It also reinforces the good news of the gospel that only divine love can explain God's will to save rebellious man. But, as the author of 2 Peter makes plain, God's love must not be construed as mere human sentimentality: a man will be saved only if he is radically changed. "It is not that the Lord is tardy in fulfilling his promise, as some think, but that he is most patient with you, because it is not his will for any to be lost, but for all to come to repentance (*metanoia*)" (2 Pt 3:9).

The second obstacle to authentic prayer is mentioned in the Matthean instruction on this subject in the Sermon on the Mount: "When you pray, do not carry on like those hypocrites, who love to stand up and pray in synagogues or on street-corners, so that people may notice them. I assure you: they have received their full reward!" (Mt 6:5). Once again, this apparently childish *ostentation* may seem too gross to be mentioned in a conference on prayer to religious. When we reflect upon the fact that the evangelist actually has in mind a certain class of people in the Christian community with which he was acquainted, it becomes clear that the issue is more subtle than it seems at first. We may note that the "hypocrites" mentioned here are a different breed from those mentioned at Mt 15:17 who have rejected the declared will of God for "mere traditions of men." The "hypocrites" in the saying on prayer *do* actually pray, but they are not immune to vanity. Their prayer is not directed solely, perhaps even primarily, to God, but to men. Hence they receive, not God's reward, but *"their* reward" (v. 6). The issue raised by Matthew concerns the difficult question of "edification," a term which now sounds so quaint, or of "witness," the more fashionable word nowadays. I should pray because I have a personal

need to speak with my "Father who is unseen," a Father
moreover "who sees what is unseen" (v. 6), who should ab-
sorb all my mind and my entire heart.

Anxiety about my life or myself constitutes a third detriment
to prayer. "I warn you," Jesus says, "to stop worrying about
your livelihood. . . . Which of you by worrying can add a single
moment to his allotted span of life? . . . What weak faith you
have! . . . Your heavenly Father realizes that you need all this
sort of thing. Aim first at seeking his kingdom and his will,
and everything else will be given to you" (Mt 6:25-33). Certain desires involve man's basic needs: food, drink, clothing;
others are illusory, like the desire to prolong one's life. What
is reprehensible, however, even where legitimate desires are
concerned, is *lack of confidence in God our Father*. Our first
concern as Christians and religious is to seek the kingdom
already incarnate in Jesus during his public ministry and now
dynamically present to the course of history in the risen Christ.
This is not to say that we have not an obligation to work, or
that we may adopt a fatalistic attitude to life, which is a pagan
outlook. Strong faith demands that awareness of our needs
never be allowed to disturb our peace of heart; it also demands great simplicity of heart. "The birds in the sky" (Mt
6:26) are by no means idle in providing for themselves. They
do however exemplify a kind of peace. The simple beauty of
"the wild lilies" growing in the fields (Mt 6:28-29) will reveal
the loving providence of their Creator not to mere lovers of
nature, but to discerning eyes of Christian faith inspired with
trust in the Father who is in heaven.

The fourth obstacle to prayer is man's almost insuperable
tendency to count upon self, remain closed within himself,
refusing to go out of himself. The self-transcendence demanded by the gospel (Mk 8:34-37) is easily displaced by
concern for self-fulfillment. Man refuses the divine challenge
to exodus! Such going out of himself produces an intolerable
feeling of insecurity. The story of the Hebrews' exodus from
Egypt illustrates this. Dissatisfied as they were by the galling
oppression of their Egyptian task-masters (Ex 2:23), no sooner
had they obtained their liberty, by God's initiative, through a

successfully engineered escape into the desert, than the Israelites were beset with that insecurity which inevitably accompanies the achievement of liberty by man. "They cried out in their terror to the Lord, and they complained to Moses, 'Were there no graves in Egypt, that you should have lured us to our death out here in the desert? Look what you have done to us by bringing us out of Egypt! Was not this what we meant, when we told you in Egypt, "Leave us alone; let us be slaves to the Egyptians"? It would have been better for us to remain slaves to the Egyptians than to die out here in the desert' " (Ex 14:10-12).

When, during Jesus' absence upon the mountain of the Transfiguration, the disciples were unable to cure a boy suffering from epilepsy, they felt their own inadequacy keenly, and in their frustration at their powerlessness in the face of this quite unexpected crisis, they turned to Jesus in bewilderment, and asked him, after he healed the child, "Why could we not cast it out?" (Mk 9:28). Perhaps they recalled the "authority over unclean spirits" (Mk 6:7-8) which Jesus had given them earlier when he sent the Twelve upon the missionary tour of Galilee. The question seems to imply a desire for some technique which *they* can work effectively. Jesus, in his reply, rebukes them for self-centeredness, of which their frustration at not being able to *do* anything is a symptom. "There is no means of casting out this sort but prayer," he says (Mk 9:29). It is by opening oneself totally to God and God's action, the essential attitude in prayer, and not by confidence in some quasi-magical skill of one's own, that the Christian will find the means to help others. Prayer that is stripped of self is the only answer to human frustration. A saying of St. Ignatius Loyola reflects this same truth: "The genuinely mortified man needs only fifteen minutes to unite himself with God in prayer." [4] The self-transcendence which is a condition *sine qua non* of Christian prayer postulates a real renunciation of confidence in self. Without that no prayer,

[4] *Fontes Narrativi De S. Ignatio De Loyola, I: Narrationes Scriptae ante Annum 1557: Monumenta Historica Societatis Iesu,* Vol. 66 (Rome, 1943).

however lengthy, can be efficacious: with it, a few moments of prayer are sufficient.

This consideration may serve as an introduction to the first facet of prayer as expression of Christian faith. Prayer is *the response to the challenge of the gospel,* to that complete reorientation of man to God in Christ, which is conversion. Here it is important to see this divine summons as an unequivocal demand for continuing conversion. The theological principle invoked by Reform theologians, *Ecclesia reformata semper est reformanda* (the Church reformed must continually undergo reform), may be paraphrased to illustrate the point. The man who has experienced conversion to God lies under obligation to work tirelessly at his conversion. St. Ignatius well understood that the *Election* in the *Spiritual Exercises,* as my response to the divine initiative, is not the matter of a moment, but the business of a lifetime. In this ongoing process, prayer appears as a necessary means to a more perfect conversion, since it is chiefly through prayer that the Christian is changed and brought into conformity with God's will in his own life. Change, as has already been noted, involves risk; at the same time, change, which is growth, is a sign of vitality.

Nowhere, as the apostolic Church well knew, was this function of prayer, as the catalyst of growth in Christian existence, so clearly exemplified as in the earthly life of Jesus, and particularly at two critical moments in his career: the struggle in Gethsemane and his last hours upon the cross. That all four evangelists appreciated the significance of these two episodes as the school of Christian prayer may be gauged by the fact that each has detected in both scenes a distinctive nuance of meaning which he has sought to express through his narratives.

Mark's description of Jesus' prayer in the garden underscores the power of prayer in bringing Jesus to accept the Father's plan for man's salvation. The evangelist is at pains to stress Jesus' state of mind as he begins his prayer. After leaving the eight behind, he attempts to communicate something of his agonized feelings to Peter, James, and John. At this point, Mark tells us, Jesus "became filled with terrified

surprise and distressed by shock" (Mk 14:33). "And he said
to them, 'My heart is near breaking with sorrow: remain here
and stay awake' " (v. 34). Withdrawing from his three dearest
friends, Jesus "collapsed upon the ground, and he began to
pray that, if it were possible, the Hour might pass him by"
(v. 35). Mark, alone of all the Gospel writers, thus sum-
marizes the theme of Jesus' prayer before he cites his words,
in order to impress his Christian reader with the tragic possibility that could result if this petition were to be granted.
All that stands between Jesus' revulsion from the Passion,
that will mean man's redemption, and his acceptance of God's
plan is the little phrase, "if it were possible."

Mark reports Jesus' words as addressing God with the term
of endearment used in Aramaic-speaking families for the
father: "Abba! (dear Father)" (Mk 14:36). Jesus, in addressing God, employs this familiar term which no Jew of the
time would dare use for fear of irreverence. Our Lord is aware
of his unique relationship as Son to God. "Dear Father! all
things are possible for you: take this cup away from me. Yet
not what I will, but what you will." Although the articulated
prayer of Jesus does not cause the heart to stop in an agony
of suspense, as did Mark's summary of the prayer, yet Jesus'
attitude is only too clear: he does not want to accept the cup
of suffering—unless such a desire runs counter to the Father's
will.

Jesus now returns, possibly to seek some comfort from his
three friends, but finds them asleep. Reproaching Simon,
he urges him to pray "that you may be spared the trial"
(v. 38). This "trial" is the great eschatological conflict between God and the forces of evil which in the biblical tradition is represented as preceding the final judgment of God.
Jesus is well aware that he is personally involved in that awful
"trial," which can only compass his own death. He then adds
the significant words, "The spirit is willing, but the flesh is
weak." "Flesh" means human nature, of course; but what
does "the spirit" mean? In the Bible it usually contains some
reference to God. If that be intended here, then the words
describe the struggle to which Jesus is subjected, torn as he is

between the Father's will and his own human reaction to the ordeal. Mark observes that when Jesus returned to prayer, "he prayed using the selfsame words" (v. 39). Does Mark hint that now there is a change in Jesus' attitude, that the new theme of his dialogue with the Father is a frank admission of the struggle between his own human weakness and openness to the Spirit of God?

Jesus returns again to find the disciples fast asleep. Mark does not record any words to them on Jesus' part: he wishes his reader to fix his attention upon the change being effected in Jesus through his prayer. When he comes back a third time he has fully accepted the Father's plan in its least detail, as may be seen from his words to the disciples: "Are you still sleeping and taking your rest? That is quite enough. The Hour has come: see, the Son of Man is being betrayed into the power of sinners. Get up! we must be on our way. . . ." (Mk 14:41-42). His prayer with the Father has transformed Jesus' attitude to his "Hour," and he embraces it with alacrity.

Matthew does not accentuate the contrast in Jesus' attitudes as dramatically as Mark. He is conscious of writing for the believing community, already aware of Jesus' identity as Son of God. He wishes to teach his reader that Christian prayer, after the example of Jesus, effects a deepening of faith's awareness that God is our Father. Matthew verbalizes Jesus' prayer in its first and second phase: both times it begins with "My Father!": "My Father, if it is possible, let this cup pass me by: however, not as I will but as you will" (Mt 26:39); "My Father, if it is not possible that this cup may pass me by, but I must drink from it, may your will be done!" (v. 42). And this attitude of acceptance, for Matthew, constitutes the motif of the third phase of the prayer of Jesus (v. 44).

Luke presents Jesus as the exemplar of victory through prayer in this critical struggle; hence, *all* the disciples are present to hear his repeated warning, "Pray constantly, that you do not become involved in the trial" (Lk 22:40, 46). The spectators observe the effect on Jesus of God's strengthening aid in the course of his "agony" or struggle (vv. 43-44). The fourth evangelist has removed the scene from "the Gar-

den," and has located it in the scene where "the Greeks" seek
out Jesus in the Temple area (Jn 12:20ff.). The incident
brings the thought of "his Hour" to Jesus' mind: "The Hour
has come for the Son of Man to be glorified" (v. 23), that
is, Jesus' Passion, with which in this Gospel Jesus' glorification begins, is imminent. "Now my soul is in turmoil! What
am I to say?—'Father, save me from this Hour'? No! it was
for this very reason that I have come to this Hour!—'Father,
glorify your name!' " (v. 28).

The second most important prayer of Jesus which is found
in the Gospels is uttered on Calvary, and we should be conscious of the fact that the evangelists have formulated that
prayer, each in his own way, to bring out a certain facet of
its significance for Christian living. Mark, followed by Matthew, stresses the awful hazard to which Jesus exposed himself in dying for us. Thus he employs the opening words of
Ps 22, "My God! my God! why have you forsaken me?"
(Mk 15:34; Mt 27:46). The Christian must expect to feel
the agonizing risk involved in total acceptance of the will of
God. The loud cry with which Jesus died remains inarticulate
in Mark and Matthew, but Luke has expressed its meaning
by the prayer, "Father! into your hands I commend my spirit"
(Lk 23:46). Jesus returns his life as his definitive gift of love
to the Father, thereby revealing the meaning of the Christian
experience of death. The scene also illustrates the peculiarly
Lucan theme of absolute renunciation as a condition of discipleship. Besides recording Jesus' saying about the necessity
of denying oneself to be accepted as his follower (Lk 9:23-25),
which is found in the other Synoptic accounts (Mk 8:34-37;
Mt 16:24-26), Luke devotes a paragraph to this doctrine
(Lk 14:25-33), which concludes with the warning, "So then
any one of you, who does not say farewell to *all* his possessions, cannot be my disciple" (Lk 14:33).

A second aspect of prayer as expression of Christian faith
is of special significance to the religious, because of the pe-
culiar risk entailed in the way of life he has chosen. Like
other Christians he strives to accept the invitation which Jesus
has issued in the gospel to all his disciples: "Be perfect as

your heavenly Father is perfect" (Mt 5:48). The religious however endeavors to reach this common Christian goal by his wholehearted acceptance and faithful use of a particular set of charisms: virginity, common life, obedience, and poverty. Within this context prayer is seen as vitally necessary to his development to spiritual adulthood, that is, to *the realization of his identity as a religious*. This means that the religious, like any other human being, must acquire in his growth to maturity a sense of responsibility toward himself, his religious family, and above all toward God in Christ.

It is often said, no doubt at times with good grounds, that certain factors in the training of religious, indeed in the structures of religious life itself, militate against such growth. As a man under this particular form of authority, the religious can tend to shuffle off responsibility by throwing it back upon his superior. It remains true indeed that in the more significant actions he performs the religious wishes to act under obedience. At the same time, faith made operative through prayer assures me that there are certain inalienable rights I can never abdicate as a mature person. By the same token there are also responsibilities for my own acts which I cannot waive. To name only the most important—no superior can go to heaven for me. No vow of obedience or of poverty, however solemn, can absolve me from the divinely imposed duty of being answerable for my own actions and decisions. The very grace of God, without which salvation is totally impossible, leaves intact that basic freedom with which a man is endowed by his Creator, and without which he could not achieve and maintain his identity as a person. "This is the word of the Lord, which came to me," says Ezekiel, " 'Son of man, what is the meaning of the proverb men repeat in the land of Israel, "Parents have eaten green grapes, and so their children's teeth are set on edge"? As I live, I swear that no longer shall there by any man among you, who will repeat this proverb in Israel. Each living person belongs to me: the life of father and son alike are mine; only he who sins shall die' " (Ez 18:1-4).

The particular set of means freely bestowed upon the re-

ligious by the God who has called him to this kind of life
demands a continual exercise of Christian faith if he is to
discover his true identity as a member of his religious family.
Admittedly, there is a truly human dignity and even natural
attractiveness perceptible in certain features of religious life.
Indeed these elements are operative to some degree in every
religious vocation. Yet it is even more apparent that, without
destroying these features, a solid growth in faith is essential
if the young religious is to discover his real identity. The
marriage of two Christians whose faith is lost or seriously
debilitated may possibly survive somehow because of the
purely human, personal love and mutual respect of the two
partners, or because of a quite natural concern and love for
the children. It is immeasurably more difficult for a religious
whose faith is not developed by prayer to find fulfillment and
meaning in his life at the merely natural level. The answer
to the question, which the great Cistercian Bernard of Claivaux
is said to have constantly asked himself, *"Bernarde, ad quid
venisti?"* (Bernard, what purpose had you in becoming a religious?), can be successfully discovered only by Christian
faith. My prayer as a religious ought to spring from a re-
membrance of my call by God, as an act of his loving kind-
ness to myself. The grateful recollection of what he has done
for me provides a kind of springboard for requesting his
further assistance in discovering and developing my life-style
as a religious. My prayer, moreover, should normally be
shaped by the special, personal relationship God has established with me by calling me to my particular religious family.
The constitutions of my religious community, which delineate
the concrete form of my religious life, provide me with the
frame of reference within which my prayer is made.

It may be useful to recall that the two qualities which the
writers of the Deuteronomic school urge as appropriate to the
prayer of Israel are (1) the active recollection (*anamnēsis*)
of God's mighty acts of self-revelation in justice and mercy
throughout the history of his people, and (2) petition made
within the covenant-relationship to which the Israelite had
been called. "Take care and be earnestly on your guard,"

Moses tells the people, "not to forget the things which your own eyes have seen. Do not allow them to slip from your heart all the days of your life. . . . There was the day on which you stood before the Lord your God at Horeb . . ." (Deut 4:9-10). Again, "Exercise diligence over yourselves lest you forget the covenant which the Lord your God made with you . . ." (Deut 4:23). These principles are concretely exemplified in the moving prayer of Solomon at the dedication of the Temple (1 Kgs 8:23ff.), in which request for God's continuing help springs from the recollection of God's covenanted promise to David.

If, as we all realize, my religious vocation is to grow in depth each day I live out my promises to God, that growth depends upon the development of my faith (as well as love and hope). Put quite simply, this means keeping green the memory of the goal to which I am called. In the *Prologue* to *The Holy Rule,* St. Benedict reminds his monks that fidelity to the religious vocation consists in a daily watchfulness and attention to the divine voice summoning them, with each new day, to a fresh response. "Let us then rise up at the voice of the Scripture, which rouses us with the words, 'It is the hour for us to rise from sleep.' And with eyes wide open to the divine light, we must hear, with vibrant ears, the warning which the voice of God gives us day by day in ringing tones, 'Today, if you should hear his voice, harden not your hearts!', and likewise, 'He who has ears to hear must listen to what the Spirit is telling the churches.' "

A third aspect of prayer as the expression of faith may be seen in that kind of prayer which springs from *the comtemplation of the earthly life of Jesus,* as it is presented in the four Gospels. The high value of this form of prayer may be readily perceived if one considers faith as an interpersonal relationship with the risen Christ—the viewpoint of St. Paul. "For me, to live is Christ" (Phil 1:21), he tells the Philippians. He writes to Galatia, "It is no longer I who live: Christ lives in me. In this present, mortal existence, I live by faith in the Son of God who loved me and handed himself over for me" (Gal 2:20). The mystery of the divine economy of salvation revealed in the gospel Paul sums up for the Colossians in a brief phrase, "Christ in you, the hope of glory" (Col 1:27). It is by means of this dynamic relationship with Christ that the Christian is made a son of God. "Through faith you are all sons of God, in union with Christ Jesus" (Gal 3:26).

The acceptance of this meaning of Christian faith, however, creates a difficulty for the thoughtful believer. How can I relate to Christ, who through death and resurrection has passed into a totally new existence, so far above and beyond me since my participation in the paschal mystery is at best inchoate and imperfect? Does not Jesus' very exaltation in glory tend to make him less real as a person, because he has passed beyond death into a life that is beyond all human experience? If I am to find a basis, common to both of us, upon which to build the relationship that is faith, it must be discovered on my present level of existence, not on that level, so far transcending my own, at which the risen Christ exists by "the glory of the Father" (Rom 6:4). If a young woman falls in love with an atomic physicist without possessing the time, talent, or interest to attain that scientific competence through which his colleagues relate to that man, it is clear—if she is to marry him and live a successful life as wife to such a scientist—that she must relate to him on some level other than that of nuclear physics. Similarly, it is only too evident that my relationship in faith with the exalted Christ must somehow be established through that level of existence, at which he found himself during his mortal life. For it was then that he most closely approximated—save for sin—my own "present, mortal existence," as Paul calls it.

Still, it would seem that the earthly life of Jesus is buried irretrievably in the distant past. What can Jesus' statement in the Fourth Gospel, "I am the Way" (Jn 14:6), made *apparently* with reference to himself during the public ministry, possibly signify for my present existence? What is the sense of the assurance Jesus gives to Philip, "The man who has seen me has seen the Father" (Jn 14:9)? If it has any meaning at all, it contains the promise that through the unique life of Jesus of Nazareth it is still possible for the man of faith to dis-

cover "the God no man has ever seen" (Jn 1:18). The author
of the Fourth Gospel himself provides a clue to the problem
in his discourse on the Bread of Life. We can obtain "eternal
life" and so fulfill "the will of the Father" on condition that
we "behold the Son and have faith in him" (Jn 6:40).

We may recall at this point a salient feature of our Gospels.
All the evangelists make it clear that the "Jesus of history,"
as modern scholars are pleased to call him, is not the *adequate*
object of Christian faith. One thing our evangelists attest un-
ambiguously: there were no Christians during Jesus' public
ministry, but only after his death and resurrection. It is only
Christ, revealed in the resurrection as Son of God, or, as Paul
says, "Son of God in power" (Rom 1:4), who can provide
sufficient grounds for the self-commitment which is Christian
faith.

At the same time, it is crucial, in the view of our evangelists, that the risen Lord is the same Person as the Jesus of
history, Jesus of Nazareth. John makes the point dramatically
in his narrative of Thomas' confrontation with the risen Jesus,
where *touching* is of such paramount interest. It is by touching
the very wounds inflicted on this body, now glorified, which
once hung upon the cross, that Thomas becomes a Christian.
"My Lord and my God!" (Jn 20:28) is proof of the fact.

I remarked earlier that the paradox of the gospel which
makes it good news is the truth it announces: that the Son of
God in glory has chosen to remain human forever. It is this
which explains why the risen Jesus is presented in the Fourth
Gospel as "the Way." It is only after he is glorified, we read
in the same Gospel, that Jesus can become the source of the
Spirit (Jn 7:37-39). "It is the Spirit that is life-giver: the flesh
profits nothing!" (Jn 6:63). This is indeed a bold statement
by the very writer who said, "The Word became flesh"
(Jn 1:14). Even "the flesh" of the Son of God does not profit
us for salvation until with his glorification Jesus can transmit
to man, through his risen flesh, the Holy Spirit. Here is the real
reason why the Son has chosen to remain human forever. "And
I, if I be lifted up, will draw all men to myself!" (Jn 12:32).

These truths enable me to see the necessity of contemplating Jesus' earthly history *as narrated in the Gospels*. On the one hand, they offer me the basis for that interpersonal relationship with Jesus which is Christian faith. For they present him, his words and actions, when he lived at the level of existence at which I now find myself, thus providing me with the possibility of relating to him. At the same time, the Gospels present him, his words and actions, not merely in their facticity, as belonging to the past, but in all their contemporary reality and significance for Christian faith. If our contemplation of the Gospels is to feed our faith, we can never afford to forget that what they record is not the precise words of Jesus (*ipsissima verba Jesu*), nor a mere factual account of what he did. They report his words and deeds as understood, interpreted, reformulated, and, above all, as *lived* by the first generation of Christians. If it is the risen flesh of Christ that gives the Spirit, it is the Spirit-filled narratives, vibrant with the living Christian faith of their authors, that make of these inspired books the privileged source for Christian contemplation. We can never afford to forget that the "Gospel truth" we are to seek in prayer, as Vatican II declares, is "that truth which God has willed to consign to the sacred books *for the sake of our salvation*" (*Dei Verbum,* n. 11). What engages, or ought to engage, our attention primarily in the contemplation of the Gospels is not scientific truth, or historical truth, or artistic truth, but *saving* truth.

One occasionally hears religious saying nowadays that to experience the presence of the risen Lord they do not find it necessary to contemplate the Gospel narratives: one simply finds the risen Christ in those with whom one lives and works. It is assuredly true that the Christian is confronted with the risen Lord of history throughout the course of his life through his relations with other men and women. The pagan also is subject to the all-pervading influence of him who is Master of history, and that even through the cultural and religious institutions of paganism. But does he recognize him? The evangelists assure us in fact that Jesus' own disciples, during his earthly life, did not pierce the mystery surrounding him. They had no Christian faith. The religious of whom we speak, of course, have Christian faith. Yet, I venture to suggest, without nourishing that faith, increasing its perceptiveness by the prayerful contemplation of the Gospels, they incur the danger of mistaking other human beings for Christ. The risen Christ is indeed *in* others: *he is not to be confused with them*. The knowledge of the risen Christ which we need as religious is not a speculative, but an existential, that is, experiential knowledge. And that comes to us most surely in prayer.

The fourth aspect of prayer as expression of faith is the vital role to be accorded *the prayer of petition* in our religious life. Not infrequently one receives the impression from spiritual writers that to ask God for what one needs, particularly if those needs be of the temporal order, is at best to be tolerated only in the spiritually unsophisticated. Once one has acquired some expertise in the life of the spirit, that type of prayer had best be forgotten. Jesus himself however insisted strongly upon petitionary prayer: "the Lord's prayer" is a series of petitions. At the Last Supper, as Jesus looks ahead to the time when the Holy Spirit will be given to the disciples, he enjoins such prayer upon them. "I assure you, whatever you ask the Father in my name he will give you. Up to the present you have not asked anything in my name. Ask and you will receive, that your joy be fulfilled. . . . On that day, you will ask in my name, but I do not say I shall ask the Father on your behalf, for the Father himself loves you . . ." (Jn 16:23-27).

I believe it is significant that Jesus urges perseverance in the prayer of petition. "Go on asking, and it will be given you; keep seeking, and you will find; knock, and the door will be opened for you. The man who persists in asking receives his request; the man who perseveres in seeking finds what he seeks; to him who continues knocking, the door will be opened" (Mt 7:7-8). The statement is unmistakably clear. Yet it appears to be contradicted by common experience. There are few among us who have not been disappointed at times in our requests to God. What then did Jesus mean? The two brief illustrations which Matthew adds to these words will clarify their sense. "Surely there is none among you, who will give his son a stone when he asks for bread, who will hand him a

serpent when he asks for fish?" (vv. 9-10). The answer to
the question lies in seeing the significance Jesus attaches to the
father-son relationship. It is in this context that he makes a
promise, which only he as Son of God can make. "If then you,
wicked as you are, know how to give good gifts to your children, how much more will your heavenly Father give good
things to those who persevere in asking him?" (v. 11). Human
parents give their children what is good for them. Yet children do not always ask for what is in their own best interest.
In that case the good parent says "No." What does the child
receive by asking, whether the request is granted or not? He
acquires by this experience a real knowledge of his relation
to father or mother. The Christian then, Jesus assures us, by
perseverance in the prayer of petition, will experience what it
means to have God as his Father.

Paul elucidates this teaching of Jesus by pointing out that
it is the Holy Spirit, dwelling within us, who is the source of
this essential experience deriving from Christian prayer of
petition. "The proof that you are sons," he writes to Galatia,
"is the fact that God has sent the Spirit of his Son into our
hearts calling 'Abba! (dear Father!)'" (Gal 4:6). "The
Spirit himself attests to our spirit that we are children of God"
(Rom 8:16). Moreover, the indwelling Spirit is able to give
us the experience of our relation to the Father as sons or
daughters, even though we may ask for what God knows is
not good for us. "The Spirit likewise comes to the aid of our
weakness, for we do not know to pray as it is necessary"—that
is to say, according to God's will. "However, the Spirit himself
intercedes through our inarticulate groans, and he who plumbs
the depths of our hearts recognizes the intent of the Spirit,
because he intercedes on behalf of God's people according to
his will" (Rom 8:26-27). It is important to realize that Paul
is speaking in this passage, not of that specially privileged experience that would be properly called mystical, but of the
ordinary prayer-experience shared by each Christian who re-
cites the *Pater noster*.

The fifth aspect of prayer as an exercise of Christian faith
is related to what has just been discussed. Faith should be

operative in our prayer so as to fill us with the conviction of being heard. A noteworthy feature of the prayer of the early Christians, witnessed to by the inspired writers, is their *intense assurance that their prayer was heard.* Indeed already in the Old Testament, God is invoked as "You who hear prayer" (Ps 65:2).

Mark employs the mysterious episode of Jesus' cursing the barren fig-tree to inculcate this doctrine. "Have faith in God," Jesus says on this occasion to the disciples, "I assure you that whoever says to this mountain, 'Get up and hurl yourself into the sea!', and does not entertain any doubt in his heart, but has faith that what he declares is happening, God will do it for him" (Mk 11:22-23). The fantastic character of the example Jesus uses only serves to underline his point that my request must be single-hearted—there can be no room for reliance on anyone except God himself. "Everything that you ask for in prayer *with faith,* you will receive" (Mt 21:22) is the Matthean version of the saying. It is surely a sweeping promise on the part of Jesus!

Luke, who does not narrate the cursing of the fig-tree, illustrates this Christian certainty of being heard in prayer by his parable about the unjust judge, utterly devoid of any religious or social sense, who nonetheless vindicates the rights of a defenseless widow because he is impelled by his own self-interest. The conclusion Jesus draws is not, as one might expect from the widow's persistence, a lesson in persevering prayer. "The Lord said, 'Observe what the unjust judge is saying. Now will not God uphold the rights of his chosen people, who cry out to him day and night, without too long delay? I tell you, he will uphold their rights promptly.—But when the Son of Man comes, will he find faith on earth?'" (Lk 18:1-8). God, the antithesis of this evil man, forced to do his duty by fear, is "the just judge of all the earth" (Gen 18:25), and he will infallibly hear the prayer of those he has himself chosen. Yet, as Jesus' final remark insists, the Christian must have complete faith that God will hear him. The vitality of such total reliance on God is in direct proportion to my self-emptying, to my refusal to put any trust in any other agency.

The sixth aspect of our topic is the *prayer of intercession,* or praying for others. This practice is an expression of our response to the "new commandment" given us by Christ, "that you love one another as I have loved you" (Jn 13:34). If a satisfactory theological explanation of the effectiveness of our prayers for others has not, to my knowledge, been discovered, the practice of intercessory prayer has a long history. The first instance of it is found in Abraham's prayer that God spare the wicked cities of the plain, Sodom and Gomorrah (Gen 18:16-33). One cannot but admire the quite uninhibited character displayed by Abraham in this dialogue with God. This artlessness and un-self-consciousness of the patriarch will be echoed in the prayers of Israel, especially in the Psalms. It is reflected in the prayers attributed to Moses (cf. Ex 33:11-13), of which Ex 5:22-23 may serve as an example: "Lord why have you inflicted disaster upon this people? and why did you ever send me on such a mission? From the time I first went to Pharaoh to speak in your name, he has abused this people of yours, and you have done nothing to rescue them!"

The most striking example of intercession is the so-called priestly prayer of Jesus in the Fourth Gospel. "Father . . . I have manifested your name to these men, whom you have given me out of the world. . . . For these I pray. . . . Father most holy, protect them with your name which you have given me, that they may be one just as we are. . . . I do not ask you to take them out of the world, but to guard them from the evil one. . . . I do not pray for these men alone. I pray also for those who will believe in me through their word, that all may be one, as you, Father, are in me, and I in you. May they also be in us, that the world may believe that you have sent me" (Jn 17:1-21).

Every prayer which Paul utters in his letters is a prayer for others (1 Thes 3:11; 5:23; 2 Thes 1:11-12; 2:16-17; Phil 1:9-11; 1 Cor 13:13; Rom 15:5-6). Almost all of them are addressed to God the Father. Paul constantly requests prayers for himself and his work from the churches he founded, and he counts heavily on their intercession for him. "Yes, rejoice

I will!" he writes from prison to Philippi, "because I know that this will result in my deliverance through your prayer and the support of the Spirit of Jesus Christ" (Phil 1:18-19).

Prayer for others is one of the truest expressions of our faith in the essentially social character of the gospel, as well as in the providence of God over all his creatures. Intercession should rank high in the priorities of any religious: the people of God evince the utmost confidence in the prayers of religious, regarding them as specially efficacious. It is plainly one of our most serious obligations to pray for those whose faith in our prayers is demonstrated by their generous support of our way of life.

The seventh aspect of prayer as expression of Christian faith is its character as *communion with the Father* through Christ in the Holy Spirit. What faith seeks ultimately through prayer is union with God our Father. "Where your treasure lies," says Jesus, "there also will your heart find its way" (Mt 6:21). "Happy the single-hearted: they will see God" (Mt 5:8). The dynamic thrust of faith expressing itself in prayer is pointed toward God. We speak quite naturally of prayer as elevation, as the raising of heart and mind to God. For faith in prayer unerringly follows the path traced out for it by Jesus in his work of redemption. "Through him," we read in Ephesians 2:18, "we both have access in one Spirit to the Father."

It was left to John, however, of all the sacred writers in the New Testament, to express most explicitly and profoundly the Christian's life of union with the Father. For John this is the dominant motif in the gospel, as can be seen from the prologue to the first epistle. "What has existed from the beginning, what we have heard, what we have seen with our own eyes, what we have contemplated and our very hands have touched—that is our theme, and it concerns the word of life. This life had been made visible . . . we here proclaim to you that eternal life, which dwelt with the Father and was made visible to us. What we have seen and heard we proclaim to you, so that you may share this life in common with us, that life of the Father and his Son Jesus Christ in which we share" (1 Jn 1:1-3).

"If a man loves me," says Jesus at the Last Supper, "he will keep my word, and my Father will love him. We shall come to him and make our home with him" (Jn 14:23). "May they all be one, as you, Father, are in me and I in you; may they also be in us" (Jn 17:21), Jesus prays.

This communion of the believer with the Father and the Son is mentioned repeatedly in 1 John. "You must then keep in your hearts that which you heard at the beginning; if what you then heard still dwells in you, you will yourselves dwell in the Son and also in the Father. And this is the promise that he himself gave us, the promise of eternal life" (1 Jn 2:24-25). "This is his command: to give our allegiance to his Son Jesus Christ and love one another as he commanded. When we keep his commands we dwell in him and he dwells in us. And this is how we can make sure that he dwells within us: we know it from the Spirit he has given us" (1 Jn 3:23-24; cf. 4:12-15). And finally, "God is love; he who dwells in love is dwelling in God, and God in him" (1 Jn 4:16).

Here ultimately faith rests, since it has found its treasure. In obedience to Jesus' bidding, it has prayed to the Father in secret, and the Father who sees what is secret has rewarded its search, or better, the Father has become its reward. The religious after leaving his daily prayer may become concerned to find he has taken no resolve, made no new plan of action. If in prayer he has learned to abide in God, if he has seen a little more clearly that God abides in him, he need have no fear, for he has discovered treasure like the man in the parable. "The man who found it," Jesus tells us, "buried it again; and for sheer joy went and sold everything he had, and bought that field" (Mt 13:44). "Where your treasure lies, there also will your heart find its way" (Mt 6:21).

Chapter 3
Religious Life as an Aïd
to the Goal of Faith

We have seen thus far that the gospel proclaims that good news which forms the foundations of Christian faith, and consequently that the gospel "is to be regarded by all religious institutes as their primary rule" (*Perfectae Caritatis,* n. 2a). We have also reflected upon the significance of prayer in the religious life inasmuch as this precious charism, a necessary concomitant of every religious vocation, is the expression of Christian faith. We now propose to assess religious life as a specific aid to the goal toward which that Christian faith, common to all believers, is orientated.

What then is the goal of Christian faith? St. Paul and St. John describe it in various ways, but both agree that it is the fullest realization of man's true relationship to God as the Father's adopted son: man's total acceptance of the will of God. It is an unfortunate consequence of that voluntarism which so deeply infected Christian spirituality, particularly that of the religious life, in the nineteenth and twentieth centuries, that our conception of the will of God has suffered a great impoverishment. Paul thinks of the will of God as the source of "your holiness" (1 Thes 4:3). By this Paul means that God desires man to share in that uniquely divine quality, holiness, which the Bible regards as distinctive of God who always remains for us "the wholly Other." The letter to the

Ephesians describes God's will as his free choice "of us in him [Christ], to be holy and innocent before him in love, by his predestining us for adoption through Jesus Christ as sons for himself" (Eph 1:4-5). For, as Paul tells the Galatians, it was "according to the will of God, also our Father" that Jesus "gave himself on account of our sins, that he might rescue us from this present wicked age" (Gal 1:4). For John, Christians "have been begotten not by the will of man, but from God," since the Word become flesh "gave to those who believe in his name, the power to become children of God" (Jn 1:21-13). "This is the will of him who sent me," Jesus announces in the Fourth Gospel, "that I should not lose even one of all he has given me, but raise all up on the last day. This in fact is the will of my Father, that everyone who beholds the Son and believes in him may have eternal life . . . " (Jn 6:39-40). This life is nothing less than "our fellowship with the Father and his Son, Jesus Christ" (1 Jn 1:3). Quite simply then, Paul and John tell us that the goal of Christian faith is to gain "access through Christ in the one Spirit to the Father," and so become "members of God's family" (Eph 2:18-19).

We may begin by noting that all Christians are called to attain this goal. "Be perfect as your heavenly Father is perfect" (Mt 5:48) was addressed by Jesus to all the disciples. It was once customary to speak of religious as those called to perfection. But that view seemed to imply that religious were a kind of elite, that there were, in short, first and second class citizens in the kingdom of God. Jesus tells us, however, that God in his relations with all men has shown himself the perfect Father; hence all are summoned to become perfect children of that Father. We must conclude then that the religious life is not something "laid on" the "ordinary" Christian life. Nor is it particularly helpful to describe the religious life as a "higher" life. Even though Paul (1 Cor 7:7a) displays a marked preference for the life of Christian virginity, following the example of Jesus himself (Mt 19:11-12), the Apostle is also aware (1 Cor 7:7b) that "each one has his own proper charism from God, one this gift, another that." It seems more appropriate, as we shall indicate later, to think of the religious life as complementary to that led by our brothers and sisters in the world. For each Christian will attain his personal perfection only in that state to which God has called him (1 Cor 7:17). Finally, it does not enhance the value or the attractiveness of the religious life to describe it as a life under vows or under a rule. To define religious life in function of these canonical realities solely, or even primarily, can create the impression that religious simply have greater possibilities for imperfection or sin than other Christians!

I venture to suggest that it is more satisfactory to think of religious life as *a distinctive manner of being a Christian.* St. Bernard, indulging in that favorite pastime of medieval men, popular (and highly imaginative) etymology, somewhere perceptively remarks that the word monk is derived from the Greek word *monos,* and hence means a fully integrated man. The religious is a Christian whose entire life, in its least details, is organized as a total response to the gospel. The religious with singular simplicity of purpose seeks to be free of those "cares" (cf. 1 Cor 7:32), to which Christian living is constantly and inevitably exposed to this world.

The nineteenth century laid great emphasis upon the differences separating the religious from other Christians. Such stress would appear today, especially since Vatican II, unnecessarily divisive, possibly even detrimental to religious as well as to the rest of the people of God. At the same time it is imperative never to permit ourselves to forget that religious life is a different form of Christian existence from that led in the world. All Christians indeed are called to perfection, that is, to the fullest possible exploitation of their baptismal grace, to total participation in the paschal mystery of Jesus' death and resurrection. The same goal is set before all; but God has provided the religious with a different set of means to reach that goal, means which not only equip him better as an individual (1 Cor 7:7), but effectively assist him as a member of his particular community by his participation in the special charism of his religious founder.

How then is religious life an aid to the goal of Christian

faith? I should like to suggest seven aspects of religious life which provide an answer to this question. In addition, I propose to describe briefly two pairs of charisms, in the order of their significance, which are essential to the religious lifestyle: virginity and common life, obedience and poverty.

The first and unquestionably the most characteristic aspect of religious life is its *eschatological polarity*, that is, its orientation to the "not yet" of Christian existence. It may be helpful to recall that the origins of religious life in any proper sense go back to the period after the liberation of the Church under Constantine around 313 A.D. Once "the Church of Martyrs" ceased to be outlawed and, in fact, became the recipient of imperial favor and largesse, certain Christians, concerned that the Church become too much at home in the world, retreated to the desert in Egypt, where they created the *vita spiritualis* (spiritual life). St. Anthony, who died in 356 A.D., thus became one of the creators of religious life. His *Life,* written by Athanasius, tells us that he drew his inspiration from the apostles, who left all to follow Jesus, and those first Christians, who "sold all their possessions and laid the proceeds at the feet of the apostles for distribution among the poor. Intent upon this idea, he [Anthony] entered the church, at the very moment, as it happened, when that part of the Gospel was being read in which he heard the Lord say to the rich man, 'If you would be perfect, go, sell what you possess and give it to the poor, and you will have treasure in heaven; and come, follow me' (Mt 19:21). As though he had received this admonition of the holy writers from God himself, Anthony . . . left the church and gave away his property . . . sold all his goods, distributing the money to the poor. . . ." The manner of life which Anthony and his disciples created spread directly to Ireland and Spain, and gradually throughout the entire Church. In the West, it was given its fundamental formulation by St. Benedict, whose influence had a lasting effect upon all subsequent founders of religious orders, including an Ignatius Loyola, whose vision was to revolutionize much of the traditional format.

We may better appreciate the orientation of the religious

life to "the treasure in heaven" by recalling the felt need which led the Church of the era of St. Anthony of Egypt to establish the feast of Christmas. Indeed, the entire Advent-Christmas-Epiphany cycle in the liturgy derives its principal motif from the same historical antecedents as monasticism. It was the concern of the Church, after her liberation by Constantine, that Christians might forget—as the Church of the Martyrs did not—the warning of her Lord to watch for his coming, since he would come like a thief in the night. The axis of this section of the liturgical year is the parousia, the second coming of our Lord in glory. The feast of Christmas is not simply a commemoration of the historical event of Jesus' birth; it is principally a celebration of the mystery of his future coming in power and glory. It summons the people of God to vigilance and hope.

Because this same orientation is a constitutive element in religious life, it looks forward in hope and watchfulness to the parousia of the risen Christ. As we observed earlier, this "coming" of Jesus, who as Lord of history is already present dynamically in the historical process, is to be understood as the complete realization of his Lordship, which remains incomplete until "he has put all his enemies beneath his feet" (1 Cor 15:25). Thus it looks forward with constancy and trust to the resurrection of the just, when "the last enemy, death" will be destroyed (v. 26). Accordingly, the theme of monastic spirituality, *fuga mundi* (the flight from the world), must retain its value, when properly comprehended, in every authentic, contemporary religious spirituality. It signifies basically the total rejection of every power structure set up in rivalry to the Lord of history. It means the adamant refusal by religious to adopt, either individually or collectively, any form of selfishness, including self-preservation, which closes a person or a community to the coming of the kingdom of God. Vatican II has alerted religious to adopt, with the Church herself, that new attitude toward the world described to some degree in *Gaudium et Spes* (n. 40). But it is imperative to bear in mind the ambivalence which the term "the world" displays in the New Testament. God indeed "loved the world" most extravagantly (Jn 3:16). Yet the same Gospel records Jesus' refusal to "pray for the world" (Jn 17:9). The evangelical truth expressed in the quaintly worded monastic theme of "flight from the world" deserves to be deeply pondered by all religious concerned with the necessary task of adaptation to modern needs and conditions. Adaptation must in fact take second place to renewal, that is to conversion, both personal and institutional, among religious. Vatican II has underlined the apostolic character of every form of religious life. Consequently, "flight from the world" can never be made an excuse for rejecting involvement in the problems of contemporary man, or for clinging to what is outmoded and refusing to adjust to much needed change. At the same time, "flight from the world" excludes any of those forms of compromise with values opposed to the gospel, to which human nature is prone. The truth enunciated by this ancient monastic theme has a special urgency in our changing world: change of heart (*metanoia*) must take precedence over every other kind of change in the mores of religious.

The second feature of religious life, which also arises from its forward-looking character and concern with the parousia, is the way in which it may be said to *exemplify that new family inaugurated by Jesus Christ as "the Last Adam"* (1 Cor 15:45). The decree *Perfectae Caritatis* takes cognizance of this aspect of religious life: "Through the impact of God's love, poured into hearts by the Holy Spirit (cf. Rom 5:5), a religious community becomes a real family gathered together in the Lord's name and filled with joy at his presence (cf. Mt 18:20). For love is the fulfillment of the law (cf. Rom 13:10), which completes and binds all together (cf. Col 3:14); because of it, we know that we have passed over from death to life (cf. 1 Jn 3:14). Indeed, such brotherly fellowship manifests the coming of Christ (cf. Jn 13:35; 17:21); it is the source of remarkable apostolic drive" (n. 15).

To assess accurately what Vatican II wishes to tell us by using the analogy of the family to designate the reality of a religious community, several points must be kept in mind. A religious family is one in which there is no father or mother, and, perhaps more significantly, in which there are no children. By this is meant that the religious community differs from its analogue, the family, in its essential character as a free society of mature, responsible persons. It is surely no secret that adulthood in the spiritual life is scarcely acquired by a man who is immature as a human being. It is regrettable that Jesus' saying about becoming like little children has so often been misinterpreted in the conduct of religious, both subjects and superiors. Actually this illustration is presented by the evangelists to inculcate two different lessons. There is the scene where Jesus blesses the children (Mk 10:15; Lk 18:17; cf. Mt 19:14). "I assure you that any man who does not accept the kingdom of God like a child will not gain entry to it," Jesus says in the Marcan version. Here Jesus insists that the openness characteristic of the child is to be understood as *selflessness,* and that this is an essential religious attitude for anyone who submits to the reign of God in his life. Matthew also transposes this imagery of the child in quite a distinctive way (Mt 18:1-3; cf. Mk 9:36-37; Lk 9:47-48). In reply to the disciples' question about status, "Who then is greatest in the kingdom of heaven?" (v. 1), Jesus states, "I assure you that unless you *turn round* and become like children, you will *not qualify* for the kingdom of heaven" (v. 3). Here the lesson is directed to all who will hold positions of responsibility in the Christian community. The expression "turn round" indicates the reversal of worldly values which should motivate the conduct of all, but especially those who are superiors in the Church. In both versions of Jesus' saying, then, the child is taken as a symbol of the radical (perhaps also of the *continuing*) conversion demanded by all who accept the gospel and mean to live by it.

Another aspect of the analogy between the religious community and the family may be helpful, especially for those religious who—not without good reason—find considerable difficulty with the application of this image to their religious congregation. The vitality of any family is assured by the fact that each of its members is at the same time a *bona fide* participant in other groups. The father belongs to the society where he earns his livelihood, the children to the society of the school, etc. The active involvement in other communities actually enriches the life of the family. Most members of a religious community simultaneously belong to other communities, professional, social, cultural. These relationships must be recognized as helpful and necessary for the life of the religious group, not as rivals for the loyalties of its members. Moreover, the openness characteristic of the ideal Christian family, by which it refuses to remain closed in upon itself in the interests of its own self-preservation, can provide a lesson to religious communities. There is still need today for the practice of a kind of "ecumenism" on the part of religious toward other groups in society or in the Church, and especially toward other religious families who need help.

To perceive the most meaningful side of the role of the religious community as a family, however, it is necessary to consider it as the exemplar of that "new family" redeemed by Jesus Christ. Part of the good news of the gospel is that Jesus actually redeemed the family as a human institution. One has only to consider the family in primitive or pagan cultures (or for that matter in the Old Testament), to realize its need of redemption. The family or clan or tribe in primitive societies tends to resist any attempt at incorporating it into the larger society of the nation or people. God's greatest miracle in the Old Testament was his creation of Israel out of the disparate Herbrew tribes, whose fierce love of their own freedom and autonomy was only overcome in the stronger solvent of faith in the one God. Even so, the history of the rupture of Solomon's kingdom after his death, like the later schism of the Samaritans, reveals how precarious that religious unity of Israel always was.

Another indication of the need for redemption, evinced by the natural institution of the family, may be seen perhaps more clearly in pagan cultures. The family looks to the past. An exaggerated "ancestor worship" can enslave the living members of a family. The son then remains inferior and subject to the father; the children, even when fully adult, are kept in tutelage to the parents.

The Gospels present Jesus as rejecting the family and clan system by word and action. The Synoptic evangelists all report the reaction of Jesus when he is told that his mother and his relatives are seeking him. "Who is my mother and who are my brothers?" Jesus asks in Mt 12:48. The evangelist continues: "And stretching his hand toward his disciples he said, 'There is my mother and my brothers. Whoever does the will of the heavenly Father, that man is brother and sister and mother to me'" (vv. 49-50; cf. Mk 3:33-35; Lk 8:21). Thus Jesus indicates his intention of founding a new family based not on natural relationships, but on the will of his Father. This same point of view is expressed by Jesus in the Lucan Gospel, where Jesus is indirectly praised by an unnamed woman who pronounces his mother truly blessed. "Happy the womb that bore you and the breasts at which you fed!" (Lk 11: 27). Jesus answered, "Rather happy are those who hear the word of God and keep it" (v. 28). That this has been the secret of our Lady's true greatness has already been made clear by Luke in his narrative of the annunciation. "And Mary said, 'I remain the servant of the Lord. May it happen to me according to your word" (Lk 1:38).

With his characteristic Christian insight into the gospel, St. Ignatius gives a certain prominence in the *Spiritual Exercises* to the Lucan episode of the finding of the child Jesus in the Temple, when he introduces the exercitant to the *Election* (cf. nn. 134-135). The reply of the twelve-year-old boy to his mother's gentle reproach "Why have you acted thus toward us?" implies Jesus' rejection of the pre-Christian view of the family and its claims. "Did you not know," he rejoins, "that it was *necessary* [that is, it was God's will] that I should be in my Father's house?" (Lk 2:48-49). To the mind of St. Ignatius, this act of leaving his parents "to devote himself exclusively to his heavenly Father's service" provides a basis for the life of "evangelical perfection."

Jesus thus liberates the family from its traditional restrictiveness and, by giving his Father's will precedence over the claims of clan, opens the family to the possibility of joining that larger society of those who seek God's will, the Church.

This is the thrust of those sayings of Jesus, which strike us as harsh. "Let the dead bury their own dead" (Mt 8:22), he tells the man who wishes to bury his father before becoming a disciple. "He who loves father or mother more than me is not worthy of me" (Mt 10:37).

Paul has drawn out the implications of Jesus' rejection of the family in favor of the will of God by proclaiming the abolition of all those distinctions, which ultimately depend upon the pre-Christian view of the family, the racial, cultural, religious differences, as well as the preferred status accorded to the man over woman. "Circumcision is nothing; lack of circumcision is nothing: what counts is keeping the commandments of God" (1 Cor 7:19). "Indeed by the one Spirit we have all been baptized into one Body, whether Jew or Greek, slave or freeman" (1 Cor 12:13). "There is no more Jew and Greek, slave and freeman, male and female, since we all are one in Christ Jesus" (Gal 3:28). "In union with Christ Jesus, neither circumcision nor the lack of it has any force, but only faith made operative through love" (Gal 5:6). "Neither circumcision nor the lack of it counts for anything, but only a new creation" (Gal 6:15). This is Paul's understanding of Christ's redemption of the family. He thinks of the whole human race as a new family in which the risen Christ appears as "the last Adam," who has become "lifegiving Spirit" (1 Cor 15:45). The divine plan for man's salvation is expressed by Paul in terms of this new family of God. "Those God foreknew, he also predestined to be remolded in the image of his Son, in order that he [the Son] might be eldest of a large family of brothers" (Rom 8:29). In this new family God alone is Father, since "it is from him alone that every family in heaven or on earth takes its name" (Eph 3:15).

The term of this redemption of the family will only happen with the full vindication of Jesus' Lordship by the overthrow of death. "Now when everything has been made subject to him, then the Son himself will be subject to him who subjected everything to him, in order that God may be all in all" (1 Cor 15:28). The human institution which is the family, like the institution of marriage, is bound inexorably to this world and subject to the regime of death. "Human beings in this world marry or are given in marriage. Those who have been judged worthy of a part in that other world and in the resurrection of the dead, do not marry. They are no longer subject to death: they are like angels. They are sons of God, because they share in the resurrection" (Lk 20: 35-36). A brief explanation of this passage which has a bearing on Luke's preference for a life of virginity (Lk 14:26) may not be out of place.

In the Bible, marriage is seen as necessary to man's existence in this present world, inasmuch as it is the means God has chosen for the preservation of the human race (Gen 1: 28), particularly after man is placed under sentence of death (Gen 3:16). Since the glorious resurrection of the just means the destruction of death (1 Cor 15:26; Apoc 21:4) for those "judged worthy of a part in that other world" of glory, marriage as we know it will have no function: its purpose will have been achieved. Luke, like Paul, associated marriage with that "outward aspect of this world which is passing off the stage" (1 Cor 7:31). Like Paul again, Luke sees a causal connection between man's adoptive sonship and his resurrection to glory (Rom 8:23). "Sons of God" is of course a familiar biblical title for the angels (Gen 6:2; Job 1:6; Pss 29:1; 89:7), who are not subject to death. Thus Luke likens the glorified human race to these members of God's family. For with the final resurrection Christ's redemption of the family will be fully realized.

Jesus created the possibility of a religious vocation by freeing the family from its ancient state of "closedness." The religious community, where the old family ties have given way to a new union of all the members, is based upon the desire to "hear the word of God and carry it out," and in this respect it exemplifies the future new family of God in Christ. It proclaims that the redemption of the family has truly been effected by Jesus' death and resurrection, inasmuch as its members have demonstrated their freedom from family ties in order to follow the will of God.

This suggests a third aspect of the religious life as *a veritable anticipation,* through "faith made operative by love" (Gal 5:6), *of man's future life* of happiness with God. This view of religious life recalls the traditional monastic theme of the *Vita angelica,* or the life in paradise. This terminology may well strike us today as naively romantic; yet it contains a truth which we cannot afford to neglect if we are to grasp the significance of the religious life. To anticipate the realization of God's Kingdom, however imperfectly, in our present existence demands the transcending of self. Jesus' requirements for discipleship make this only too clear. "If anyone wishes to come after me, he must say 'No' to self, take up his cross, and follow me. For whoever wishes to save his own life will destroy it: whoever will destroy his own life for the sake of the gospel will save it" (Mk 8:34-35). Jesus shows how fully aware he is of the magnitude of this demand: he knows that a man's life is worth more to him than mastery of the entire world. Indeed he asserts that there is nothing that could render such an exchange equitable—except being his disciple. "What use would it be for a man to acquire the whole world and suffer the loss of his own life? What could a man give in exchange for his life?" (vv. 36-37). In the Fourth Gospel, this demand of Jesus is restated in terms of the paschal mystery, accomplished first in Jesus himself and then, necessarily, in every Christian. There the theme "through death to life" is stated more positively by means of a brief parable about sowing (Jn 12:24-26). "Unless the grain of wheat, when it falls into the ground, dies, it remains in isolation; but if it dies, it yields great fruit. He who loves his own life destroys it, while he who hates his own life *in this world* will guard it for eternal life." Here Jesus speaks primarily of himself, of his own death and resurrection. But he at once indicates that this pattern must be reproduced in every authentically Christian life. "If a man serves me, he must follow me; and where I am there also shall my servant be. If a man serves me, my Father will honor him."

The message is all too clear: I can become a disciple of Jesus in the full sense of that word, when at last, by the Christian experience of death, I return my life as a gift to God my Father in token of my filial love and obedience to his will. This is what the paschal mystery of man's redemption required of Jesus himself. He redeemed rebellious man by accepting in love his own death and resurrection, as the Father willed, since thereby he gave his human life to God in acknowledgment of man's relationship to him as his Father. The wonder of our redemption in Christ is that he has made of death, the one universal, inexorable necessity for all living beings, *the means* to man's salvation from death. In Christ, death has been made the path to life!

The Christian realizes, no less than the thoughtful pagan, that death is an experience which each human being must face alone, stripped of all he has come to value in this life. No accumulation of material things can give man security against death. There is no human love powerful enough to ward off from the beloved death's inevitability. No man is so much captain of his own soul that he must not capitulate before death's demands. But for the Christian, who answers the invitation to become a disciple of Jesus Christ, who has gone through death to life with God, the sting of death has been drawn, death's victory has been turned to defeat (1 Cor 15:55).

The religious has chosen a way of life, which anticipates— insofar as it is possible—this liberating experience of Christian death. He refuses to seek security in the amassing of possessions. He renounces joyfully the precious experience of loving and being loved by another human being, of perpetuating himself in children. He is content to relinquish into the hands of other human beings the specific determination of his own career, his own life. The religious does these things in love and freedom to anticipate the total self-giving required of every Christian in the hour of his death. Yet the wise religious knows that this gift is not made perfectly in any single instant: it must be offered again and again with increasing love for God and neighbor. "We know," says St. John, "that we have passed from death to life, because we love the brotherhood" (1 Jn 3:14). To the extent that the religious makes this self-oblation out of love for others, he may truly be said to "have passed from death to life."

The fourth quality of the religious life is its *openness to the Spirit of God,* its charismatic character. This quality is notably present in the charism given the founder of a religious order, a charism which must be safeguarded by the fidelity of all the members in carrying on the particular purpose contained in the founder's vision. For that reason Vatican II urges on all religious as part of their renewal "a continuous return . . . to the original vision that inspired their institute" (*Perfectae Caritatis,* n. 2).

It may be indeed that this charismatic quality has become obscured in our religious life, because of the assimilation of its structures to the hierarchical forms of government within the Church. The result has been that the various relationships, which constitute a religious institute (the very term is symptomatic), have come to be considered chiefly in terms of those juridical realities, upon which they are in part undoubtedly founded (e.g., jurisdiction, canonical appointment, exemption—even vow). *Lumen Gentium* would appear to correct this situation by pointing out that "the way of life arising from the response to the evangelical counsels does not form part of the hierarchical structure of the Church." On the other hand, "it is inextricably bound up with her life and holiness" (n. 44). The history of the origins of the religious life has much to teach the religious community of today in its search for self-identity.

We may select some random examples. Originally, the superior was quite simply the spiritual father of his community. That meant he was a "superior person" by reason of his endowment with those charismatic gifts of direction and discernment, so essential to anyone seeking to lead a life of open-hearted responsiveness to the Holy Spirit. The views of the Abbot Pachomius, creator of religious community life in the proper sense, are enlightening. For Pachomius, the authority of the superior arose from the nature of his function as symbol of the presence of Christ at the head of his Church and of God's dominion over his people (cf. Placide Deseille,

O.C.S.O., "Origines de la vie religieuse," *Lumière et Vie* 9 [1970], 28). The submission and mutual service of the religious within the community was looked upon as a favored means to the purification of the heart so basic to a life of dedication to the Spirit.

There is a paragraph in Paul's letter to Galatia, which appears to have inspired this conception of religious life. "My meaning is this: live under the guidance of the Spirit, and you will refuse to yield to the solicitations of your lower nature. . . . If you are led by the Spirit, you are no longer subject to law. . . . The harvest of the Spirit consists in love, joy, peace, steadfast endurance, kindliness, goodness, faithfulness, gentleness, chastity. And law has no place in a life of this kind. Those who belong to Christ's party have crucified that lower nature with its passions and solicitations. If our life springs from the Spirit, the Spirit must direct our living" (Gal 5:16-25).

From this it becomes evident that the vitality and esprit de corps of a religious family depend primarily upon the constancy and intensity with which its members correspond with the graces, with which God has chosen to endow them by giving them their religious vocation. Because these Christians have been favored with similar charisms, and not because of any organizational efficiency or juridical authority, they possess true union with one another. Mutual love prompts them to assist one another in the continuing quest for God through a kind of "conspiracy of wills" inspired by the divinely given attraction toward a common, specific goal.

All this presupposes that openness to the Spirit of God remains a salient feature of religious life. Such openness demands Christian discernment in perceiving and carrying out the will of God in one's personal life and in the orientation of the community. Acquisition of the art of discernment is not as easy as much contemporary writing would lead one to imagine, and amateurism in this delicate area becomes increasingly common—and harmful. To distinguish successfully between the voice of God and my own egotism, between the power of the Spirit and the tyranny of group power-politics, the religious must discipline himself through self-abnegation. What is possibly even more difficult—the community *as a group* must practice abnegation. Group despotism is scarcely to be preferred to the old-fashioned autocracy of the individual superior.

Since we propose to discuss presently those specific charisms which constitute the religious vocation, we may now turn to the fifth aspect of religious life, its *contemplative character.* While it is true that most Christians are drawn to the religious state because they seek closer union with God in prayer, the term "contemplative" is not employed here in this narrow sense. More broadly it includes every kind of attention to God and to his action in our lives, as well as in contemporary events within the Church or in the world. The cultivation of this contemplative habit of mind demands some sort of withdrawal, at least from time to time, in order to discover or recover one's right direction, to assist growth in the Spirit, or to be alone with God.

The Gospel records have preserved the tradition of a practice of this kind in the public life of Jesus himself. Mark explicitly notes the prayer of Jesus on only three occasions (Mk 1:45; 6:46; 14:35). Yet he mentions other occasions when Jesus withdrew in order to be alone (Mk 1:12; 3:13; 9:2) in the desert or upon the mountain. The evangelist Luke has associated these moments of withdrawal with Jesus' habit of prayer: at his baptism (Lk 3:21), in the midst of his ministry (Lk 5:16), before choosing the Twelve (Lk 6:12), before Peter's profession of faith (Lk 9:18), at his Transfiguration (Lk 9:28), on the occasion of his teaching the Twelve to pray (Lk 11:1).

These episodes in the Gospels seem to support the high esteem in which silence has always been held in religious life, and to suggest the positive values attaching to its practice. The aim was surely never merely to create a vacuum, but rather to promote this contemplative quality of religious life, which we are considering. This purpose governed the almost automatic movement to the desert, undertaken by the founders of monasticism. The retreat to the desert was motivated by a desire to find God, not by anti-social tendencies. Today, when the traditional, institutionalized forms of silence seem to have disappeared from religious houses, communities should seriously ask themselves what effective aids to recollection must be substituted for it.

It is significant that in this age filled with the clamor of voices the Church has made space in the Eucharistic liturgy for moments of silent prayer. Not a few religious congregations have established—oddly enough from the traditional point of view—a "house of prayer" where its members may withdraw periodically to enjoy quiet communion with God. The growing practice of "renewal weekends" for religious is another indication of our increasing awareness of the value of silence and reflection. One is tempted to predict a return to some modified form of the ancient discipline—at least when religious have been disillusioned sufficiently by the restless turbulence of an era of transition.

The sixth quality of religious life is its *apostolic spirit*. Every religious, even the cloistered monk or nun, is a person chosen to be sent upon a mission. While it is true that every charism is given to the person as an individual, not to communities, it is also true that these graces are given for the good of the whole Church. The very social character of Christianity itself demands concern for others. When St. Ignatius Loyola was first asked about his aim in founding the Society, he simply said "to save people" (*salvare animas*). The religious, perhaps even more than other Christians, ought to be conscious of his need to save himself by saving others. Nor should he permit himself to see any conflict between these two purposes. "We know what love is by this," says John, "that Christ laid down his life for us. So we in our turn are bound to lay down our lives for our brothers" (1 Jn 3:16). Paul considers that his own salvation is bound up with that of his converts. "For after all," he writes to the Thessalonians, "what hope or joy or crown of pride is there for us, what indeed but you, when we stand before our Lord Jesus at his coming?" (1 Thes 2:19). We religious cannot afford to forget that the charisms with which we have been graced as

religious imply—in addition to a personal gift to ourselves—
a sending to others.

This may serve to introduce the seventh aspect of the religious life: its *role in the edification of the Church,* or, in
more contemporary phraseology, its witness-value. Vatican
II takes cognizance of this function. "The life led in response
to the counsels of the gospel thus appears as a sign which
can and should draw all the members of the Church to a ready
and effectual fulfillment of the duties of their Christian vocation" (*Lumen Gentium,* n. 44). The term "edification" has
been deliberately employed above, because it is a significant
word in Paul's vocabulary, where it is related to the "building
up" of the Church. While he uses it in a transferred sense, the
original meaning is still perceptible. Jesus had promised that
he would "build up" his Church with Peter as rock or foundation (Mt 16:18). Paul's criterion for judging the relative
value of the charisms given the Corinthian community by the
Holy Spirit is their effectiveness in "building up" the community. "You are, I know, eager for gifts of the Spirit; then aspire
above all to excel in those which build up the Church" (1 Cor
14:12). His esteem of prophecy rests upon his conviction that
"prophecy builds up a Christian community" (1 Cor 14:4).
The highest gift of all is love, since "it is love that builds" (1
Cor 8:1). Indeed, the Church, of which Christ is head,
"builds itself up by love" (Eph 4:16).

In his closing words to the community at Thessalonica
Paul says, "Therefore hearten one another, build one another
up—as indeed you do!" (1 Thes 5:11). It is to be noted that
this Pauline word is applicable only within the Christian
Church, since it presupposes faith. While Paul is concerned
for the conversion of the pagans (cf. 1 Cor 14: 20-25), he
never speaks of "building them up." Thus the witness given
by religious is directed first of all to other Christians. Their
devotedness and fidelity, above all consecrated virginity,
must speak to married Christians to "build up" the inviola-
bility and sanctity of that union. The openness and universality
of love displayed by a religious community, where union of
hearts is founded not on personal preference but on a common

quest for God, is a living reminder to the Christian family not to close itself to the larger family of the Church. The tractableness and expendability of the witness given by religious to those in authority in the Church recall Jesus' injunction that ecclesiastical authority must be deployed as service to the people of God.

Here it may not be inappropriate to remind ourselves of the reciprocal nature of this "building up" within the Church. The witness of married Christians tells the religious that the detachment and mobility accompanying a life of virginity are meant to expand the heart by a truly universal love and apostolic concern for all. The witness of the single life led by some Christians in the world recalls to religious the total trust in God's provident care and the limitless generosity in sacrificing one's self, required of him by the evangelical counsels. It is imperative that we appreciate the complementarity found in the various kinds of Christian testimony, which function for the "building up" of the whole Church. It is instructive to recall that Christian virginity is mentioned, both in the words of Jesus and of Paul, in the context of their teaching on Christian marriage (cf. Mt 19:11-12; 1 Cor 7:25-34).

We have already considered one of the very precious charisms, prayer, which forms part of the divine gifts comprising a religious vocation. It now remains to reflect upon those four charisms which are most commonly thought to constitute religious life. As has already been suggested, these gifts may be conveniently described by pairing religious chastity with community, poverty with obedience. Of these four distinctive graces, the charism of virginity is the most fundamental to the religious state. All other features of this way of life have been subject to modification throughout history: the cenobitical or community life could always be abandoned for the eremetical, or life of solitude; the specific modes of practicing poverty and obedience are relative to the particular aim of each institute. It is the grace of religious virginity, which has been singled out by Vatican II as "an outstanding gift of grace" (*Perfectae Caritatis,* n. 12), because it allows of no modification, and it has in fact been regarded from the birth of religious life in the Church as its essential characteristic.

Christian virginity is presented already in the New Testament as the special sign of God's favor, since it graced the earthly existence of Jesus himself as well as the life of the Mother of God. Indeed, even though virginity was not included as an ideal in the spirituality of Israel, the Old Testament occasionally gives testimony to its excellence. The prophet Jeremiah represents redeemed Israel as "the virgin daughter of Sion" (cf Jer 31:4, 21). Christian esteem for the virginal life has been inspired by the example of our Lord's total self-dedication to God. Matthew reports Jesus' declaration that this state requires a special gift of God himself. "It is not everyone who can accept that, but only those to whom God has granted it" (Mt 19:11).

Mary's virginity appears in the New Testament as one of the ancient beliefs of the apostolic Church. Indeed, this article of faith is one of the very few facts on which the Infancy narratives of Matthew and Luke are in accord (cf. Mt 1:16, 18, 20, 23, 25; Lk 1:27, 34, 35). Matthew emphasizes this belief by associating mother and child repeatedly (Mt 2:11, 13, 14, 20, 21), in spite of the prominence of St. Joseph in all these episodes. In the dialogue between Gabriel and Mary which Luke has constructed, we find a remark which scarcely makes sense, as long as it is considered a factual statement, made in an historical situation by Mary. "How will this happen since I do not know any man?" (Lk 1:34). If, as many commentators agree, the tense of the verb "know" is to be construed as future ("since I shall not know any man"), this is a declaration of an intention not to marry. Yet Mary is already "betrothed to a man by the name of Joseph" (v. 26). However, when the sentence is understood as an assertion made by Luke to his Christian reader of the belief of the Church in the perpetual virginity of Mary, the puzzle is solved. The evangelist Mark may perhaps be considered, in his turn, to give testimony to the virginal conception and birth of Jesus, when, in the scene of Jesus' rejection in Nazareth, this writer identifies him as "the son of Mary" (Mk 6:3)—an unusual form of designation among semitic peoples. In view of the testimony provided by the New Testament to the early Church's veneration of Mary as the virginal "mother of Jesus" (cf. also Jn 2:1; 19:25; Lk 1:43), it is scarcely to be wondered at that devotion to our Lady has always been cherished by those Christian men and women who have consecrated their chastity to God.

Paul clearly shows a preference for the celibate life, and thereby gives evidence—rare enough in his writings—of his familiarity with the sayings of Jesus. "I should like everyone to live as I do myself, but each has his own charism from God" (1 Cor 7:7). The profession of religious chastity, in fact, proclaims God's "graciousness" in his election of the Christian people. If a man wishes to know concretely what the grace of God means, he has only to look at the lives of those who have accepted the grace of Christian virginity as their most significant response to God's call.

The author of the Apocalypse represents as virgins the faithful Christians who have given their life in testimony of their fidelity to the gospel (Apoc 14:1-5). The witness of religious chastity reminds all Christians of the essentially virginal character of every Christian life. It is a sign of total personal fidelity to Christ and of that selfless, always growing love for all Christ's members, affirmed by every authentic Christian life.

Virginity is also revered as "a singular sign" (*Perfectae Caritatis,* n. 12) of the contemplative element, implied in the gift of Christian faith, which is the response to Jesus' warning to "watch" for his future coming, "like a thief in the night" (1 Thes 5:2, Lk 12:39-40; Apoc 3:3; 16:15; 2 Pt 3:10). For while it is undoubtedly true that the first Christians took for granted the imminence of the parousia, the multiple testimony by the sacred writers to the authenticity of this saying of Jesus indicates a vivid awareness that no one really knew the time of his coming. The Matthean parable of the Ten Virgins (Mt 25:1-13), who are, collectively, the bride of the parousiac Christ, graphically presents this Christian duty of watchfulness. Indeed, it is not perhaps implausible to discern an allegorizing trait in the strange detail that all the virgins *as a group* are affianced to the bridegroom. If this be intentional on Matthew's part, it may reflect the presence in some early Christian churches of a kind of prototype of communities of religious.

The religious life is not, like marriage, a sacrament. May not the explanation given by ancient monastic writers for this be correct—namely, that the perfect observance of Christian virginity offers the fullest possible realization in this present life of the grace of Christian baptism?

From the beginnings of religious life in the Church, the practice of Christian virginity was usually set within the context of community life. This was true even of those who ultimately answered the call to the eremetical life. For it was only after he had proven his spiritual maturity for a considerable period, by living as a cenobite, that the monk was permitted to advance to the solitary life and to battle alone with Satan.

Two reasons may be discerned in the writings of the Fathers for this conjunction of religious chastity and common life. Both are understood as responses to Jesus' commandment that we should love one another. Life in community assists the intensification of the spirit of mutual service, while virginity permits the approximation of that universal charity, displayed by the blessed in heaven. The sharing of all earthly goods in common is like chastity a sign of total Christian abnegation of the self.

Many religious nowadays are preoccupied with the definition of "community." Perhaps in the past it was too facilely assumed that the careful delimitation of a certain area where religious spent their lives was sufficient to create community and make its reality perceptible. Sociologists explain the origin of the town wall or hedge as an attempt by primitive man to draw a magic circle round a group of dwellings in order to keep out evil spirits. By now it should be obvious that the erection of a cloister grille does not effectively constitute, or promote community. It is perhaps not quite so obvious to many religious that a majority vote does not create consensus.

Can one indicate the elements which create community? Certainly, solidarity in a common enterprise whose success is of real concern to all the partners is one factor. My grandmother used to say that "a parish without any debt was a very poor parish indeed!" The most important formative factor in the establishment and continuing vitality of a religious community is undoubtedly the sharing of a common spiritual experience. If I may be forgiven a reference to my own religious family—a common misapprehension not infrequently voiced about the Jesuits is that they "have no community life." To those who hold this opinion, the esprit de corps which the Society is considered to exhibit is a mystery. This closely knit fraternity has confessedly few of the "traditional" means of institutionalizing community. But its "sense of family" springs from the experience of the *Spiritual Exercises* shared by all the members. In fact, the Constitutions of the Society are nothing but a distillation within a different frame of reference of the same spirit.

As was implied earlier, a religious family must be open-ended like the Church itself: on condition that he believe, no man is barred from it.

Community life provides the balance that is needed in a life consecrated to Christian virginity. The bachelor and the old maid have never been thought to furnish the ideal of a thoroughly human existence. "It is not good for man to be alone," said the Lord God at the commencement of human history (Gen 2:18). Indeed, it is the presence of the religious community that assists and assures the attainment by the individual of the difficult goal of self-transcendence. "Self-fulfillment is not simply an affair of freedom, but also an affair of community," John Courtney Murray once wrote. "Briefly, self-fulfillment is the achievement of freedom for communion with others" (*America*, December 3, 1966). I suspect that St. John Berchmans meant much the same when he said, "Common life is my greatest mortification." He does not appear to have had such a low idea of community life as to consider it merely a curb upon originality, nor such a high idea of it as to consider it irreformable. Rather he appears to have esteemed the voices of the community as a continuing invitation to Christian self-transcendence.

Since, as we have observed, the goal of the religious life is the maximum exploitation of the grace of Christian baptism, it will be useful to recall Paul's conception of that sacrament. "You must realize," he wrote to the Roman church, "that we who have been baptized into Christ Jesus have been baptized into his death. We were buried together with him through baptism into his death in order that, just as Christ was raised from death through the glory of the Father, so we also might begin to live a new kind of life" (Rom 6:3-4). Paul considers baptism the rite of initiation into the Christian community: accordingly, he stresses the sacramental experience of our union with the death of Jesus. With his characteristic insight he has seen that the ticket of entry into Christian fellowship is death to selfishness. The religious finds assistance from the community for self-transcendence in proportion as he dies in Christ to that old self.

But we must describe this role of religious common life more positively. *Perfectae Caritatis* reminds us all "that chastity is practiced with greater security, where a real sense of community flourishes upon the genuine brotherly love reciprocated by all the members" (n. 12). The community assists the religious, who has consecrated his chastity to God, to grow in love for all men through the truly Christian charity it offers him by its unaffected interest in his work, its concern for his successes and failures, and the sense of security and solidarity it provides by its wholehearted acceptance of him as a person. These sincere overtures made by Christian charity to the individual religious sustain the feeling of belonging that enables him to live at peace. It certainly springs from no natural source, but has its origin in "the love God has shown us in Christ Jesus our Lord" (Rom 8:39). *Congregavit nos in unum Christi amor!*

It is well to remember that the religious community is a fellowship of persons. Although unity in the congregations he founded appears as a perpetual concern in Paul's letters, it is to be observed that the word "unity" is only rarely employed

by him (Eph 4:3,13). Instead, he habitually uses by preference a term which means "communion" or "fellowship"
(*koinōnia*). He considers the call to Christian faith a summons from God, "who has called you into fellowship with his
Son Jesus Christ our Lord" (1 Cor 1:9). Paul writes to Phile-
mon: "[I pray] that your fellowship [with me] in faith may
become operative in a more profound appreciation of every
blessing, that our union in Christ brings" (Phlm 6). Paul
is always intensely aware that this oneness in Christ is a true
communion between persons.

This same sensitivity to the personal character of Christian
fellowship appears in Paul's celebrated description of the
Church as Christ's Body. "Just as the body is one and has
many members, and all the members of the body, many
though they are, form one body, so also is Christ. . . . Indeed, the body consists of not one but many members. If the
foot were to say, 'Since I am not a hand, I do not belong to
the body,' it does, for all that, still belong to the body. If
the ear were to say, 'Since I am not an eye, I do not belong
to the body,' it does, for all that, still belong to the body.
If the body were all eye, where would be its hearing? If it
were all hearing, where would be its sense of smell? As it is,
God has set each organ or limb in the body as he willed"
(1 Cor 12:12-18). Paul's point is that it is the very variety
of function or part which constitutes the unity of the whole
body. We should reflect upon what this means for the union
of Christians in the Church: it is *that very aspect of an individual which makes him distinctive*—that is, a person—
which creates and sustains Christian fellowship. The same
principle must be allowed to operate in a religious community.
What contributes to the vitality of our common life is the
unique contribution of himself that only each person can make
out of Christian love for the entire fraternity.

The dynamic source of this religious fellowship is the risen
Christ who makes his presence felt most fundamentally in the
gospel and in the celebration of the Eucharist. It would scarcely
be an exaggeration to say that the celebration of the Eucharistic liturgy provides the primary reason for the existence of any

religious community. The summary description in the Acts of the Apostles of the daily life of the earliest Christian church in Jerusalem has been considered the exemplar of all religious families, since the days of St. Anthony of Egypt. Vatican II has drawn our attention to this ancient tradition and its relevance today. "A robust sense of community must be maintained, after the example of the primitive Church, where in the entire group of the faithful, there was but one heart and one soul (cf. Acts 4:32). Now, as then, the same means are to be employed: the gospel teaching, the sacred liturgy—especially that of the Eucharist, prayer, and fellowship in the same spirit (cf. Acts 2:42)" (*Perfectae Caritatis,* n. 15).

The evangelist Luke says of the primitive church of Jerusalem, "They were persevering in their attention to the teaching of the apostles, the common life, the breaking of the bread, and prayers" (Acts 2:42). He would seem to tell us that what inspired their constancy in sharing all their earthly goods with one another (vv. 44-45), what lent joy to their common meals, was the exposition of the gospel by the apostles and, above all, the Eucharist. It was the unifying force of the word of God that had created Israel and renewed its unity at critical moments throughout its history. At the foot of Sinai, Moses, we are told, "took the book of the covenant and read it aloud to the people" (Ex 24:7), to give them a sense of their new identity as the people of God. After the return of the Jews from the Babylonian exile, "Ezra the priest brought the law before the assembly, consisting of every man and woman, and anyone capable of understanding what he heard. He read from it . . . from early morning until midday. . . . All the people listened attentively to the book of the law" (Neh 8:2-3). Thus the chosen people regained their sense of solidarity after their return to the homeland from half a century of exile.

The hearing of the gospel proclaimed in the liturgy is calculated to give the religious community a renewed sense of its solidarity, making each member conscious of his shortcomings, reminding him of the grace of his vocation, inspiring him to respond more fully to the love manifested by his confreres. "Every inspired scripture is useful for teaching, refuting error, for the reform of manners and training in right living, so that the man of God may be proficient and equipped for good work of every kind" (2 Tim 3:16-17).

The Eucharistic action is in fact creative of community. "Because there is one bread, we, though many, are one body, since we all partake of the one bread" (1 Cor 10:17), says Paul. Another remark of his shows the particular appropriateness of the Eucharist for inspiring the religious with the radical orientation of his life to the parousia. "As often as you eat this bread and drink from the cup, you proclaim the death of the Lord, until he comes" (1 Cor 11:26). As the sacramental anticipation of the coming in glory of the risen Christ, the Eucharistic liturgy is a daily reminder of that watchfulness and longing for the second coming which has inspired religious life from its beginnings.

It remains to consider briefly the two charisms of religious poverty and obedience. Attention has already been drawn to the relative character of each of these aspects of religious life. Poverty, both personal and collective, and the practice of obedience are determined by the constitutions of each religious institute, in accordance with its own specific goals. In addition, the sign-value of poverty is also relative to the cultural and economic conditions of time and place. The current problem which besets almost all religious families is how to find a meaningful and authentic expression of the ideal represented by religious poverty within our contemporary culture. Poverty is essentially a religious and Christian attitude—not to be confused with economy. The desideratum is to discover how best, in our necessary relationships with the material world, to nurture and intensify in ourselves, as individuals and as a community, total abandonment to the providence of God. In our pursuit of this difficult enterprise, it is well to recall that some kind of deprivation, consonant with the apostolic work of the religious order, is a staunch ally.

Once again, the chief source of inspiration for cultivating this virtue, which history shows to be a reliable measure of the spiritual health and fervor of a religious family, is the

Bible. The "poor of God" (*'anawim*) became an ideal in
Israel during the Babylonian captivity and after the return of
the people to Palestine. It was only in her hour of defeat,
humiliation, and exile that Israel learned to place all her
trust and hope in her God. Through the teaching of her
prophets, she came to see that her security lay only in the
divine will, and in her active cooperation with the divine plan
for the salvation of mankind. Gradually she recognized that
the covenant God had made with her was a responsibility
no less than a privilege.

Jesus demanded this consciousness of man's absolute need
of God as a necessary condition for the acceptance of God's
kingdom, or reign in history. "Happy the poor in spirit: theirs
is the kingdom of heaven" (Mt 5:3). By his attribution to
our Lady of the *Magnificat* (Lk 1:46-55), Luke presents the
mother of Jesus as the embodiment of this biblical ideal and
implies that it explains, in part, the place of privilege which
Mary had already been accorded in the faith and devotion
of the earliest Christian communities.

I venture to suggest that Paul's characteristic doctrine of
justification by faith is simply an application of this same
principle of seeking our security in God alone. "Being then
justified by faith, we possess peace with God through our Lord
Jesus Christ, through whom we have also gained access to the
grace in which we now stand, and we rest our security upon
the hope of the glory of God" (Rom 5:1-2). Paul's use of the
metaphor of "boasting" (almost exclusively his in the New
Testament) serves to indicate how highly this man, inclined
by temperament to boast, prized this attitude (Phil 1:26;
3:3; 2 Cor 10:17, 18; Gal 6:4; Rom 3:27; 15:17).

Paul moreover finds it congenial to present Christ's work
of redemption in terms of his willing acceptance of poverty.
It is adequately expressed by the stark phrase, "he emptied
himself" (Phil 2:7). Our redeemer is he "who being rich
became poor for your sake, in order that you might, by his
poverty, become enriched" (2 Cor 8:9).

These last texts suggest a significant theme that is not ab-
sent from the ideal of religious poverty. The religious has

committed himself, through his acceptance of this charism, to identify himself and his institute with the whole human family, inasmuch as it exhibits its poverty, in manifold ways, before God. In addition to the more obvious form of deprivation, the lack of material goods, there is the poverty of ignorance, of insecurity, of loneliness, of illness, of failure, above all, the poverty of sinfulness. By giving gratis and generously what he himself has received as gifts from God, the religious endeavors to carry out creatively the command of Jesus. "You have received without paying: you must give without charge" (Mt 10:8).

Someone once described the ideal of religious poverty as "being happy with nothing." The accent here falls upon the attitude of joyousness for the Christian, who seeks to emulate the empty-handedness of Jesus upon the cross, who has surrendered everything to the Father, in giving himself for all men.

It is perhaps the charism of religious obedience which presents the greatest problem for the contemporary religious. There is a *practical* difficulty, arising from the fact that we live in a society whose ideal is democracy, whereas the traditional concept of religious obedience was created in a patriarchal society, one in which the patriarchal tradition was honored. In that tradition the superior was regarded as the person who had all the ideas because he was, or was deemed to be, a superior person. Today we are inclined to consider the complexity of directing any organization the size of a religious community, to feel that the responsibility for decisions must be spread among a committee, or extended in certain instances to the whole group. What then becomes of the religious obedience owed to the superior?

There is also a theoretical, or better, a *theological* problem, which is more keenly felt in our age than formerly. In what sense, apart from the canonical or juridical reality of his appointment, can the superior be said to be in the place of Christ? We are realists enough to be aware that, like ourselves, the superior is prone to err in his assessment of any given situation. How then is it consonant with man's dignity as a person to submit his judgment, and, as St. Ignatius insists, even his understanding, to that of a fallible human being in the name of religion?

The practical problem is perhaps more easily solved. It is surely the part of prudence for any superior to involve as many of his subjects as he can in the process leading to decision. Where a decision involves a single individual, that individual should be urged to present his reaction to a project which concerns himself or the community. In his celebrated letter on obedience, St. Ignatius insists that the subject has a duty to make known to his superior his own judgment and feelings, particularly the repugnances he experiences to the proposed course of action.

In an instance where the decision involves the community or the whole religious family, it seems to be only common sense to solicit the views of as many as possible. Centuries ago, St. Benedict insisted that the abbot should summon his entire community to advise him on any major concern, adding the discerning observation: "The reason we have said that all are to be called to the meeting is that often the Lord reveals the better course of action to a younger member" (*The Holy Rule*, n. 3). The same paragraph, however, reminds the community that the ultimate decision rests with the superior, "that all may obey him in what he has judged more opportune."

In an age of committees and assemblies, which seeks to involve the whole religious family in what is termed the "decision-making process," it becomes easier to forget this truth, once obvious and accepted, that the superior is the one to make the final decision. Father Daniel Lord, S.J. once defined religious obedience as "controlled initiative." This appears to be a satisfactory description of religious obedience, inasmuch as it takes account both of the active participation of the subject in a decision-making process and of the primacy of the superior, to whom ultimately decision belongs.

The theological problem is admittedly much more difficult. I have but two observations. It is not quite exact to say the superior takes the place of God, or of Christ. No human being can ever accept, much less demand, the total gift of self which the believer owes to God alone. The remark cited by Luke, "He who hears you hears me; he who despises you despises

me; and he who despises me despises him that sent me"
(Lk 10:16), refers simply to that authority present in the
preacher of the gospel conferred upon him for his task by
Christ and by the Father—as the immediate context shows.
The obedience which the religious gives his superior is a symbol, however, of that obedience owed uniquely to God. Religious obedience is a concrete sign to the world that I am a
follower of Christ, that I am totally dedicated to pursuing the
will of God.

My second observation is that religious obedience is a special case of that discernment, which we have seen to be necessary in the charismatic existence which is the religious life. In
any significant decision in my religious life, I seek to find
concretely what is God's will for me here and now. This question I attempt to answer with the assistance of the superior.
An important presupposition is that both of us must practice
discernment to make a prudent decision. In many, perhaps
most, instances, the superior will be able to guide me because
of his expertise in discerning, or because of his more com-
prehensive or objective view of the situation. It may happen,
however, that the solution given by the superior is not as
adequate or as good as my own. In that case, when I obey
I attest my willingness to commit myself to God in Christ,
making my act of obedience a symbol of my total dedication.

Our review of the various helps to growth in Christian faith,
provided by the religious life, appropriately concludes with
obedience, which without question is the most efficacious stim-
ulus to this development. Paul, as we have seen, thinks of
the response of faith as obedience (Rom 1:5; 15:18). And
John never tires of insisting that to love is to obey (Jn 14:15,
23; 1 Jn 5:3; 2 Jn 6), and that such obedience is the necessary condition for union with Christ and the Father (Jn 15:10;
1 Jn 3:24). The obedience of which these two inspired writers
speak is, of course, that rendered to God and to Christ. Yet
what they assert about the intertwining connections between
faith, love, obedience, and union with God, provides a starting
point for the concept of religious obedience, which finds its
ultimate justification in its function as a sign and pledge of
these realities.

Conclusions

It has been traditional in Catholic theology to speak of the religious life, not without justification, as the way of the "evangelical counsels." The expression implies a distinctive manner of being a Christian, which is however firmly rooted in the gospel. To an earlier age, less critical perhaps than ours (as we like to think) in its interpretation of the New Testament, it was self-evident that certain incidents in Jesus' earthly life provided the bases for the salient features of the religious life. Thus, for instance, the story of the rich young man (Mt 19:16-29), who sadly refused Jesus' invitation to "sell all," was regarded as the scriptural justification of religious poverty. In fact, as early as the days of St. Cyprian, who in 249 A.D. wrote a treatise on Christian virginity, it is possible to discover citations of all those passages which have since become *loci classici* on this subject (Mt 19:10-12; Lk 20:31-36; 1 Cor 7:32-34; Apoc 14:1-4). The rule of St. Benedict finds support for the prescription of monastic manual labor (*The Holy Rule,* n. 48) in the examples given by "our fathers and the apostles"—an allusion, no doubt, to the communal living of the primitive Jerusalem church (cf. Acts 2:44-47) and to the practice of Paul (cf. 1 Cor 9:12; 2 Cor 11:9).

Today's more sophisticated approach to the Gospels has called in doubt the validity of some of these appeals to the Scriptures. In fact, a methodology of this kind now appears questionable, because of its over-literal, fundamentalist tendencies. Accordingly, it seems preferable to explain the phenomenon of the religious life rather as a most original and creative response, by groups of Christians, to the dynamic operation of the Holy Spirit within the Church. So far as concerns her hierarchical structuring, the Church emerges in history integral and complete without this particular modality of Christian life. The invention of religious life was not the result, then, of any necessity springing from the nature of the Church; rather, it was the somewhat imaginative achievement of Christian magnanimity, desirous of following a way of life that is "beyond the gospel." It might be more accurate to say that religious life was born of a response to the gospel pushed to its human limits by the Spirit of God. If the diagnosis be a correct one, it should cause no surprise that most attempts to justify this free creation of the Christian spirit by invoking texts of Scripture is destined to encounter refractory difficulties, if not outright failure.

I may be permitted here to refer to a recent remark of Michel Rondet, the distinguished French Jesuit authority on spirituality, which in my opinion gives a profound insight into the problem of relating the religious life to the New Testament. He suggests that, instead of attempting to define or justify it in terms of "the application of evangelical counsels, somehow traceable to the letter of the New Testament," it is eminently more satisfactory to envisage it as "the fruit of a highly original reading of the gospel, that has gradually acquired precision through fidelity to the powerful dynamic of the Sermon on the Mount" ("Signification ecclésiologique de la vie religieuse," *Lumière et Vie* 9 [1970] 142).

This conception of the origins of religious life prompts the reflection that one serious obstacle to the success of its renovation today may lie in our misapprehension of the vital and dynamic character of the evangelical traditions upon which it is founded. The Matthean parable of the Talents (Mt 24:14-30) appears to suggest that the transmission of the Christian faith entails risk. The man who buried the money entrusted to him did so, on his own admission, because he refused to trust his master, with the result that he actually defrauded him through his own hypercautiousness. There are those in the Church for whom "maximum security" is the prime consideration in handing on "the deposit of faith," so that to transpose it from a mode of thought that is called "perennial," or to reformulate it in any other language than the one which is unchangeable (because dead) is censured as a betrayal. This was certainly not the attitude evinced by Pope John XXIII in his opening speech to the Second Vatican Council. "Our duty does not lie merely in guarding this precious treasure as though we were concerned exclusively with antiquity. We must dedicate ourselves with alacrity and intrepidity to the task which the present age lays upon us. . . . The substance of the ancient teaching contained in the deposit of faith is one thing: the formulation in which it has been enshrined is quite another." This serenely courageous attitude of an octogenarian pope reflects none of the derring-do of the mere innovator; neither does it find congenial the timorousness or triumphalism of those whom it dubbed (in the same speech) "prophets of doom."

I believe it is not an exaggeration to say that the dynamism of Christian faith entails an invitation to risk. This is particularly true of that vocation to a living of the gospel, freely permitted and endorsed by the Church, yet not strictly necessary to her existence. Still, it is a question, even here, of a *calculated risk*. Origen's self-mutilation has always been regarded as a misguided interpretation of the saying about cutting out an organ that is a source of scandal!

It is here that the discernment of spirits, long practiced in the Church and so sanely and simply codified by St. Ignatius Loyola, finds a significant place in *aggiornamento*. As far as our religious renewal is concerned, the second set of rules in the *Spiritual Exercises* "for a more accurate discernment of spirits" (nn. 328-336) are specially appropriate. For these formulate a diagnostic for "those who seek to rise in the service of God our Lord to greater perfection," and are intended to train in spiritual discretion the man whose magnanimity of response may tend toward an exaggerated or fallacious zeal. For it ought now to be manifest to all who have seriously engaged in the spiritual renewal of their religious institute that not everything that is new is to be adopted, nor all that is old is outmoded, and hence to be discarded. It would seem to be simply common sense that nothing should be abandoned in the traditions of a religious family, until its original purpose is comprehended and appreciated, *and* before what is to be substituted in place of it is clearly perceived and subjected to scrutiny.

In this context, the relevance of Christian faith becomes evident. For faith functions as the discerning eye of Christian love. Without these, there can be no hope of an authentic renewal of the religious life. Where they are operative, its adaptation to the contemporary needs of God's people without the neglect or destruction of what is traditionally sound is assured.